KU-674-092

PREACHING THROUGH THE CHRISTIAN YEAR

4

Sermon outlines for the seasons of the Church's Year

Fenton Morley

MOWBRAYS
LONDON & OXFORD

© *Fenton Morley 1974*

First Published 1974
by A. R. Mowbray & Co. Ltd
The Alden Press. Osney Mead
Oxford; OX2 oEG

ISBN 0 264 66115 X

Text set in 12 pt. Monotype Bembo, printed by letterpress,
and bound in Great Britain at The Pitman Press, Bath

PREFACE

What is the use of a sermon? According to 2 Timothy 4.2, Saint Paul would say that it is a means—though not the only one—whereby we are to 'preach the word: be instant in season, out of season; reprove, rebuke, exhort, with all patience and doctrine.'

One function of the sermon of particular relevance to our contemporary situation is what might be described as 'illumination'. It is the preacher's responsibility to illuminate for himself and for others what are the main issues of the Gospel and of life as people have to live it. I have attempted to do this in these sermon outlines rather than to offer a comprehensive treatment of any of the themes selected. They are intended, after all, to be only launching platforms for other people's exploration of theology.

I am grateful to my wife who has typed the whole of this in manuscript. I dedicate this book to her and to all wives of clergy and ministers, who have heard their husband's sermons, and anecdotes, without complaint during many years of partnership in ministry. So doing, they have manifested all nine of the Gifts of the Spirit!

Salisbury 1974   *Fenton Morley*

CONTENTS

INTRODUCTION

There are no two preachers exactly alike, for preaching calls for the exercise of individuality. Likewise those who favour a monochrome Church in the interests of Church unity are mistaken: there must be diversity within the unity, if it is to be a unity of the Spirit, for the Spirit does not diminish individuality, but rather heightens it. And God's created order, which is the work of the immanent divine Spirit, is nowhere uniform but multiform. When therefore the Spirit of God utters the creative word of God through preachers, we must expect those preachers to differ to a marked degree from each other. This must not of course be out of alignment with 'the paradosis'. The preacher must deliver to others what he has himself received. But if he uses the individual gifts with which God has endowed him, he will proclaim *fresh things* from the treasure house of the Christian faith, though not brand new things and not novelties. He will commend old truths in a new way, and the newness and the freshness will stem largely from the uniqueness of the preacher's own personality.

The writer of this book of outline sermons, the fourth in our series called *Preaching through the Christian Year*, is a strong personality. Fenton Morley, formerly Vicar of Leeds is now Dean of Salisbury. The Christian public will not think first of Fenton Morley as a preacher, for they will connect his name with *Partners in Ministry* (1967), the most radical report on the payment and deployment of the clergy of the Church of England for centuries. This was the work of a Commission appointed by the Archbishops of Canterbury and York, of which Fenton Morley was Chairman.

Fenton Morley is not just an able administrator and a dignitary of the Church. He is at heart a parish priest: he understands and loves people, of all sorts and he has the ability to make personal contact with them very quickly. All his movements are quick and purposeful, yet he is warm and friendly. He is dignified (as a Dean should be) but does not stand on ceremony. A prodigious worker, ready to surmount barriers, with wide experience not only in Britain but overseas, and backed by an excellent academic record. After I had first met him I was interested to learn that he was born and bred in Merthyr Tydfil and faced life first the hard way against the background of the great depression.

This book which he has produced under my general editorship is what you would expect: direct, down-to-earth, competent and concise. He does not pack too much into a sermon (a fatal mistake) and he keeps each sermon to one theme able to be summarised neatly and sometimes intriguingly into an overall title like 'The Patron Saint of Doubt' and 'The First Christian in Europe'. If some might say that Fenton Morley's preaching is not rhetorical in style, it would have warmed the hearts of the Apostles ('Lord now speakest thou plainly and speakest no proverb'), because this preacher does speak plainly. And he expects good works to follow and accompany faith.

Here is preaching within the compass of the average parish priest who is prepared to work at his sermons and make these outlines his own. Herein lies the supreme value of this fourth book in our series. It is a book for the man who wants to be a better pastor in his preaching. He will be wise therefore to take it up, buy it, and use it. And not only he, but his congregation will profit and be better grounded in 'the faith once delivered to all the saints'.

D. W. Cleverley Ford

ADVENT

Tomorrow's world

The path of history is strewn with blueprints of the future. Some of them have ranked among the classics of literature. Such were Plato's *Republic*, Saint Augustine's *City of God*, Bacon's *New Atlantis* and More's *Utopia*. These were predominantly optimistic pictures of ideal states from which present evils could be eliminated.

In the last century, however, there has been a change of mood. H. G. Wells, G. B. Shaw and Aldous Huxley were less sure that the future would be better than the present. George Orwell's *1984* was a terrifying projection of contemporary trends.

Man's increasing mastery of his universe is reflected in popular television programmes. The prophecies of science-fiction, many of which have in the past had an uncanny knack of coming true, take modern inventions a step further. What kind of world do they forecast?

1. *The Universe ahead*

The general picture is of a universe of inter-planetary exploration. On earth, science controls man's environment. He has become a city-dweller. His manual labour is reduced to a minimum. But he is going to be conditioned and educated and selected for specific functions in the community.

His every physical and material want is met. But one is not so sure about his deeper needs. For his world seems curiously dull, impersonal and meaningless. Life requires little effort or sacrifice. The senses are satisfied but the personality seems frustrated. Morals are practically non-existent in respect of personal relationships. Religion appears to have disappeared, to be replaced by astrological and other cults providing emotional or aesthetic satisfaction.

But conflict remains. Most contemporary prophets seem to assume that in the world of the future there will be tension and strife, perhaps on a global or even inter-planetary scale. For however firmly they predict changes in man's environment, none of them dare to predict equal changes in man himself.

One is reminded of the story of the porters on an expedition attempting to hurry through the African bush who put down their loads and refused to go any further. They said: 'We have come so far and so fast, we must now wait for our souls to catch up with us'.

What really matters most is not so much Tomorrow's World as Tomorrow's People who will inhabit it.

2. *The Christian Concern*

How do Christians view this question of the future, with hope or with despair? It depends to some extent on how they view 'the world'. There are two attitudes to this in the New Testament. One sees it as fundamentally opposed to God and the source of evil. The other describes the world as the object of God's love. For its sake He had sent His Son into human life. Then, particularly in the Johannine tradition, the hope of the future is of God saying 'behold I will make all things new' with a new world in which pain and sorrow are done away and the Tabernacle of God is with man. It is a world of new people, renewed by God's love and grace. And it is not only a vision for the future. The new life begins now.

But it is the other view to which not a few Christians incline, either by apathy or through despair. Some almost hope for some awful cataclysm which will leave only a pre-selected and saintly minority to start again in another Eden—and to produce another Cain. What we have to recognise is that the future is being shaped now. We have to accept some measure of responsibility towards it as part of our discipleship and ministry.

3. *Ministry to the future*

That ministry is defined in the Anglican ordination service. The new priests are bidden to be 'messengers, watchmen and stewards of the Lord.' And that applies to all Christians, to be . . .

Watchmen—aware of and sensitive to the trends in human society, trying to understand what is happening in science, in politics, in economics and every development that affects people.

Messengers—people with a message of truth speaking to people in terms relevant to their situation, illuminating the issues bearing upon the decisions which have to be taken.

Stewards—accountable to God and accepting responsibility however irresponsible may be our society.

For the Christian dare not despair about the future or be afraid of it. He cannot be cynical about human frailty or credulous about human perfectibility. Because he has faith in God, he can have faith in man under God. He faces the crises of tomorrow knowing that crisis means danger but also opportunity. Because he says 'Yes' to God, he can say 'Yes' to life. And he knows that tomorrow's world is being shaped today and he is involved in the shaping of it.

ADVENT

The book of hope

WHY READ THE BIBLE?

That is a fair question and there are many answers to it. But the basic answer was given over four hundred years ago in 1549 by the author of the Prayer Book Collect for what has come to be known as 'Bible Sunday', the second Sunday in Advent. He wrote: 'Blessed Lord, who hast caused all Holy Scriptures to be written for our learning; Grant that we may in such wise hear them, read, mark, learn, and inwardly digest them, that by patience, and comfort of Thy Holy Word, we may embrace, and ever hold fast the blessed hope of everlasting life, which Thou hast given us in our Saviour Jesus Christ.' In other words, we read the Bible so that we may have hope.

1. *Hope in the Old Testament*

The theme of hope runs through the story of Israel. It stands out in the response of Abraham to the call of God and in Moses' leadership of the people from Egypt through the Wilderness to the Promised Land. Later the Psalmist repeatedly referred to the Exodus to prove his point that as God had acted to save Israel in the past, He could be relied upon to act again. Even when the prophets denounced the sins of Israel, they could hold out the hope of God's forgiveness if His people would repent. When Jeremiah realised that the political future of Jerusalem was hopeless, he never lost his hope in an ultimate restoration of the true Israel. And even more significantly he was convinced that there would be a new relationship between God and man based upon an inward and individual covenant. In the servant theme of Isaiah we find the highest expression of hope in the Old Testament in the concept of Redemption through vicarious suffering for others. For the ground of hope in the Old Covenant is not based upon man's capabilities but upon the nature of God, His loving-kindness and mercy as well as His justice.

2. The Hope in Christ

It was not easy for the people of his time to realise that their ancient hope was being fulfilled in Christ. They looked for political liberation and economic security and vengeance on their enemies. What Jesus was offering them was what the Collect calls 'The blessed hope of everlasting life', and this was not what they wanted. It was not so much 'everlasting life' as 'eternal life'—the life of God's eternal kingdom. This was a new dimension of living and a new freedom from slavery to fear and to sin. It meant a new sonship which looked to a loving Father with complete trust and obedience. It set a man in a context of loving relationships with others. It enabled him to rise above his circumstances and face the future with confidence. It asked of a man himself the total response of faith to the Grace of God.

This is the hope which Christ brought by His teaching. His person and His work. In a word, it was Salvation and it is the hope which runs through the New Testament. But to understand this we must see it not as a doctrine but as an experience shown in the life-situations of individuals, groups and churches.

3. The Life-Situation

The importance of this life-situation approach to the Bible is worth underlining. We have to try to put ourselves in the situation of the people who heard Jesus and 'companied with him'. We have to read the Epistles as they were first intended, as personal letters to our own church in its local context. If we do that, then it quickly becomes apparent that their problems are our problems today. For we too are a minority movement facing the pressures of a civilisation which leaves God out of account and wants to treat man as merely a functional unit. We too are a church with tensions and conflicts like those of Galatia and Corinth. And the last chapters of St Paul's Epistles which so often deal with the problems of family life can speak cogently to our circumstances in the home. Above all, as millions have found throughout the centuries, when the individual comes to read the Word with sincere expectation and an open-minded readiness to be shewn the truth about himself, he will not be disappointed. For this is the Word from the Father who cares about his 'life-situation' too.

So to the question 'Why read the Bible?', the answer 'Because it is the Book of Hope' is a valid one. The theme of the Bible is that God is and God acts and God cares. And it dares to answer the question of the ages—'What is Man?'—by affirming that Man is no less than the Child of God . . . sinful, but saveable. Because of that it can face man's future with hope.

ADVENT

What do you hope for?

1. *Hope from the stars*

Alexander Pope wrote:
  'Hope springs eternal in the human breast:
  Man never is, but always to be, blessed.'
Man is always hopeful. But the objects of his hope change from one age to another and sometimes they take curious forms. Nowadays many people set their hope on the stars. Our mass-circulation newspapers and magazines respond to consumer-demand by giving up considerable space to astrological forecasts read by millions. What matters is not so much whether people take these 'seriously' as the fact that they are prepared to think that the lives of individuals can be influenced by the movements of distant inanimate bodies. Part of the attractiveness of astrology is that it satisfies a need to find design, meaning and power in life and offers a ground for hope. For the forecasts are always optimistic. They dare not be otherwise.

2. *The gambling hope*

Something to hope for . . . this is the need which lies also behind the extraordinary extension of the craze for gambling. It used to be dismissed as an addiction of the stupid and ignorant or a harmless indulgence of the wealthy. It has now become a major industry and socially acceptable for all classes. It can be argued that it meets a need. For when life is dull and predictable, gambling gives one an excuse to dream about something which might happen to transform one's circumstances from outside.

Both gambling and astrology can be fairly criticised as irresponsible and irrational and spurious attempts to meet this human need. Nevertheless the success of their appeal challenges Christians to consider whether their Gospel offers a hope which is genuine and adequate.

3. *The Gospel hope*

There is no doubt that many were attracted to Jesus expecting a fulfilment of their hopes. Some were disappointed that he did not satisfy their political and revolutionary expectation. But others including social outcasts found in him a promise of new meaning and purpose. A few got through to the heart of his message which was that men could hope for God's grace to act within their lives not merely outside in their circumstances. In this lay the real hope for the world as a whole, and it was embodied in Christ himself.

But that hope seemed to die on Good Friday. It could not have revived unless there had been an utterly convincing experience of the Risen Christ. Now there was hope that even death itself had been defeated. The Church became a community of people for whom hope had been realised, at least during its first stage. They went on expecting Jesus to return again in power and did not recognise that he had indeed come in the power of the Spirit. They had to adjust themselves to going on living in the ordinary world. They had to provide the structures necessary to a continuing Church—an organised ministry, written records and standards of organisation and conduct. They had to change the focus of their expectation from an event in the future to a Person in the present— to Jesus in his Body the Church.

4. *The hope today*

The Second Coming is still part of Christian hope but now in a different context. Jesus told his disciples not to speculate about the times and methods of God's action. Neither must we. Instead we live with a hope based on fact and faith. For the Christian hope is basically an attitude to life, to people and to God. It expects change but primarily change in oneself and in other people. It regards no person and no situation as absolutely hopeless. It is concerned to bring hope to those who have no hope—and that can call for a revolutionary concern and action springing from deep compassion and responsible involvement.

So in a world where men may snatch at spurious hopes, or lapse into despair and cynicism, the Christian cannot keep his hope to himself. He has to share with others his experience of God's power to help man to deal effectively with the human situation. And that must be evident in the life of the local church as well as in the personal relationships of the individual Christian. It is there that people must be able to see that 'with God all things are possible'.

CHRISTMAS

Let Christ in

It was Christmas Eve. The Midnight Eucharist was being televised from Southwark Cathedral near London Bridge. As the broadcast began, a million viewers heard a thunderous knocking on the great door of the Cathedral. It was accompanied by a voice shouting 'Let me in!'

The interruption came from an old tramp. He had been sleeping rough, under a nearby railway arch. Awakened by the sound of music and by the lights of the Cathedral, he demanded to be let in out of the cold. He seemed to express the demand of the poor and needy of the world to be let in to our celebration of Christmas.

That is a demand of which people today are more aware than were previous generations. The hungry and homeless millions are making their presence felt. Hundreds of charities make a 'Christmas Appeal' because they know that at this season most people are willing to recognise their involvement in the needs of others. They are ready to let the world in and perhaps to acknowledge how at the first Christmas the Saviour of the world was identified with the under-privileged. For he too was one for whom there was no room at the inn. He began his life with no advantage of status or wealth or material security.

1. *The Christ outside*

Letting the poor in . . . perhaps. But there is a barrier to letting Christ in. We have commercialised Christmas and sentimentalised it. A glamorised Bethlehem scene has become only an ornament. So history repeats itself. The early Christians chose this day for their festival because they hoped to distract men from the heathen Saturnalia which took place at this time of the year. But the old heathen ways fought back and still do so.

What is at stake is the commemoration of Christmas as the Birthday of the Son of God. To keep it as only a season of 'goodwill' and jovial self-indulgence, even of family fellowship, is missing the real meaning of the divine truth which gives the real and lasting joy of Christmas. What is that truth?

2. *What Christmas says about God*

The New Testament sees the first Christmas as unique evidence of the character of God. Previously He had revealed Himself through

9

people and through events. Now He showed Himself completely in the Person of Jesus.

The method of God's self-revelation is considered especially in the early chapters of the Gospels of St Luke, St Matthew and St John, and in some of St Paul's letters. That Christians of those days accepted without question an Incarnation and a Virgin Birth is in itself remarkable. Jewish Christians would never have fabricated such a story if they were trying to convince fellow-Jews of Jesus' Messiahship. Nor would they have invented it for their Gentile audiences. Greeks were already familiar with legends of children of divine origin, born as a result of liaisons between gods and mortals. They would have been all too ready to interpret an Incarnation in similar terms. In any case, in the early days of Christian preaching, the doctrine did not figure prominently because the preachers were more concerned with Christ's return than with his origin.

When they did formulate the doctrine it was the fruit of their understanding of what Christ had been and of how God had acted. This was the principle of Incarnation which is vitally important to the Gospel. It is crucial to our understanding of prayer and sacrament.

3. *What Christmas says about Man*

But the Gospels saw that first Christmas as a revelation of humanity as well as of divinity. Christ entered human life not just to give us great teaching and wonderful example. He came to bring men back into union with God and to give them power to overcome the sin which was the man-made barrier against the Father. He came into their life to redeem it from within and into a human family to give family life itself a new dimension of relationship in love.

In Him the divine and the human were so united that his disciples knew him as one wholly integrated person. That he never appeared to them to sin, did not minimise his humanity for them. He had not assumed a sinful human nature because sin is no part of true human nature.

So we have to see in Christmas the 'joyful mystery' of the divine and the human. And in a sense this is an Incarnation which never ends. For it is something which happens in each of us. We have within us the divine and the human. This is the inescapable tension of the Christian life but it can be a creative tension if, over and over in life, we are prepared to put aside other things, as the shepherds

did, and say with all our heart . . . 'Let us now go even unto Bethlehem and see this thing which is come to pass, which the Lord hath
made known unto us.'

CHRISTMAS

Christmas keeps on changing

'Christmas is not what it was when I was young'. But it never is!
The festival has a curious capacity for retaining traditions going
back through the centuries and at the same time changing almost
imperceptibly.

Behind some of the traditional observances lay customs now
almost forgotten. The coins in the Christmas pudding and the
indispensable Christmas cake go back to ancient times. The coins
were originally a bean, a pea and a clove and whoever found them
in the Twelfth Night Cake would be respectively king, queen and
jester presiding over the revels. And the revels went back to the
Roman Saturnalia which the Christian festival tried to displace.

The mistletoe was the pagan protection against lightning.
Mince pies were reminders of the spices brought by the Wise Men.
The Christmas Crib takes us back to the thirteenth century.
St Francis devised it to recall people to the simplicity of the first
Christmas.

The celebration of the festival went on changing. In 1652 the
Puritans tried to abolish it by Act of Parliament. A century and a
half ago, an American poem brought the fur-clad figure of Father
Christmas and his reindeer into the picture. A few years later the
first Christmas card appeared. At about the same time Queen
Victoria's husband, Prince Albert, brought the Christmas tree
into this country from Germany.

So it goes on. Every year the festival changes a little, yet every
year traditional elements remain. Nowadays its observance seems
to start earlier and we have given up the celebration of the full
twelve days of Christmas, so dear to our forefathers.

Perhaps we are nowadays more self-conscious about celebrating
quite so self-indulgently as in the past and speaking so confidently
about peace and goodwill. We are uncomfortably aware that there
is so much starvation and homelessness, and so much conflict. Yet
this might be bringing us past all the glamour of Christmas to the

real heart of the matter. For its real meaning says something to us about the bare essentials of humanity, reminding us too that while there was no glamour in the first Christmas, there was certainly glory.

1. *And it came to pass . . .*

Bethlehem was a place of meeting. Mary and Joseph came 55 miles to Jerusalem and then another five to the village where Joseph had to register for the census. The inn was probably a caravanserai like the one shown to pilgrims today as the Inn of the Good Samaritan on the Jericho road. It would be like an open square courtyard, walled-in on all four sides. The people could sleep under the lean-to roof against the walls, with their animals tethered in the middle or in the stable space at the far end. The large gate-way would be securely bolted and barred against marauders. Because there was no room in the sleeping space in the inn, Mary and Joseph had to spend the night with the animals, while the families and commercial travellers, merchants and perhaps soldiers, slept in some measure of comfort. For a caravanserai was a place where people of many different backgrounds and nationalities took shelter together.

And there was another meeting, so the narrative says, with the shepherds from the fields down in the valley. They said they had seen a vision of glory and joy when they had been on a nightshift guarding their flocks. They had come to see for themselves the child whom they had been told to identify by the fact that he was laid in a manger.

Yet another meeting was to take place later, the story goes on. This time—perhaps many days afterwards—a group of foreigners arrived, astrologers from the East, searching with strange intensity for a child of mysterious origin and curious destiny. They came, marvelled, and disappeared as quickly as they had come.

Last of all, says tradition, came soldiers bent on the destruction of all recently-born boy babies. But the child had gone.

2. *The place of meeting*

There is movement and meeting in the Gospel description of the first Christmas. We make it a static scene and so lose its meaning. Ecclesiastical art through the centuries has been unable to resist glamorising the stable until it becomes a palace. This is unfortunate but it is understandable that men should want to express their sense of wonder at the Incarnation, in elaborate terms. But this has served to obscure the real wonder of the Event which is independent of human glorification. St John's Gospel has no account of Bethlehem. Instead he tells how the Word became Flesh and dwelt among us. It is as though his mind was reaching upward past all the conventional observances of the Birth to think about its meaning from the godward aspect.

3. *The place of beginning*

Again in St John's Gospel in the first chapter, the author quickly sweeps on to the manhood of Jesus, the Light of the World. But we tend to stop short at Bethlehem as if the stable were the end of the story. There are many people who do just this. They are willing to rejoice over the birth of the Babe, but not to face him as the Man who has grown up. In a sense, they are like the parents and godparents who want to have a child christened but see that event as the end of the child's religious life.

But the message of Christmas was of Emmanuel—that is, of 'God with us'—throughout the whole of life. The peace and goodwill of God was not confined to Bethlehem. It was active in Nazareth, in Galilee, in Jerusalem and in those last awful hours on Calvary. If we fail to recognise this, then our religion is a kindergarten exercise, not lived out in mature and adult life.

Yet during the life of Jesus one can see the meeting which began at Bethlehem going on and developing. It is a meeting of the world which has no room for Jesus with the Saviour who is content to begin life in a stable. It is a meeting of men at work, with a vision of the reality behind the scene of material activity. It is a meeting of people who are concerned about the future and about the problems of humanity, with the Christ who is the answer to their questions.

The Passion of Calvary is the Passion of Bethlehem. The Glory which began at Bethlehem is the Glory of Easter. 'Behold the Babe' becomes 'Behold the Man'.

NEW YEAR

The family diary

Next to the Bible, the most important book in our home is what we call The Family Diary. It is nothing much to look at—simply a small leather-covered notebook about an inch thick. But it contains the record of the main events of each year since my wife and I were married. At least, that was how it began.

We put into it the things which happen in any family—births, when the baby cut the first tooth, when the children started school, college or university, confirmations, those illnesses which the school medical authorities ask questions about years after they have happened, the examination results that seemed momentous at the time. Then there are also the dates and places of holidays, details of when we bought the car or the washing machine or the fridge, and of course the notes of total income each year. That last piece of information has been useful. It was always discussed with the children so that they knew just what was left to be allocated to pocket-money or extras. Incidentally, they took for granted that children knew their parents' income and were rather surprised when they found that other children had no idea of the financial position in their own families.

When we started this many years ago we had accidentally left a page or two blank at the beginning. This now contains the Family Tree, as far back as we can discover it. There are no splendid names or colourful escutcheons, just farmers and seafarers and engineers and a Welsh bard or two. But youngsters take a great interest in this kind of information. They want to know something about their roots. So does an increasing number of people today, if one is to judge by the growing flood of enquiries about genealogies received by churches with ancient registers. Perhaps in an impersonal and rootless age, people want to know more about their own identity and want to feel a sense of belonging.

1. *The value of retrospect*

The above is simply a personal illustration of the value of the advice given in Deuteronomy 8.2 to 'remember all the way'. All the way, and not just the highlights of it. And the first thing one is compelled to recognise is what one owes to people who have been one's companions on the way, and not only those to whom one is most indebted within the immediate circle of the family. One was a Saint unrecognised at the time, but looking back one is aware of her quiet goodness, that glorious sense of humour, the way in which she ignored her own physical condition to look after the sick. There were sinners too like the man who seemed to be simply and utterly perverse, damping all enthusiasm, the kind of 'touchy

Christian' who takes offence where none is intended. But we remember how we came to learn of the load he was carrying at home with a child in mental ill-health.

The Diary becomes like a collection of Pauline Epistles each with its postscript of gratitude to God for people. Paul could dare to remind some of his leaders of their indebtedness to himself. This one cannot do for oneself. All that is possible is a prayer that something has been of value and service to others. God knows all about that.

2. *What really happened*

One thing which a diary like this does is to help one to attain a sense of proportion. Turn back the pages a few years and here is a time which one would prefer to forget. There was suffering or failure, loneliness or fear. If one had known what was ahead when it began, it would have seemed impossible to bear. But somehow it was endured. The journey was like the one in Psalm 84.6 of the man who 'passed through the valley of misery and used it for a well and the pools were filled with water.' It did not seem like that at the time. But looking back one can see that strength was coming from somewhere. Perhaps as the Psalmist said of the wayfarer in this verse quoted: 'His strength was in God'.

At least all this enables one to look somewhat more objectively at present troubles and to see them in the perspective of the way so far. This is a ground of confidence and hope.

3. *To see oneself*

But retrospect can prick any bubble of conceit. It makes us realise that, as Wordsworth wrote. 'The Child is father of the Man.' In fact the Man never gets all that far away from the Child. We recognise the continuity of the inner self and the disquieting persistence of attitude and outlook. The same basic problems of relationships seem to recur. We have learned so much about life from the long journey of experience. But we seem to learn so little about ourselves except when we stop to look back with as much honesty as we can achieve. We may then realise that regret is not enough. What appears to be necessary is what the New Testament calls 'metanoia', meaning a complete change of mind, not just the old mind given an annual spring-clean. This is the repentance which would give us the renewal we know we still need, however many years have been recorded in that Diary.

4. *The way ahead*

There are blank pages in the Family Diary waiting to be filled perhaps more by what will happen in the lives of children and grandchildren than in one's own life. Nevertheless those blank pages and the record of the past are reminders of one great theme which runs through the New Testament. That is the concept of the stewardship of time. It stands in complete contrast to any contemporary denigration of time as unimportant which shows itself when we do things 'to kill time'. For the Christians of those days had a sense of accountability to God for every day. They lived with a kind of urgency without haste. They looked hopefully towards the future and were aware of eternity. But they felt that NOW was the day of salvation and opportunity. They were creating tomorrow by what they were doing and being today. They began each day with prayer that they might use it to God's glory and they planned ahead with His guidance. And they did this together so that the book of their lives was not a collection of individual biographies, but a truly 'family' diary. And this is exactly the impression left on the reader by the Acts of the Apostles. This is the book of the Family of God, with all the problems and joys which an ordinary family can experience, as they travel all the way together, made one in Christ.

EPIPHANY

Christ in the family

THE BOY OF TWELVE

The Gospels are not biographies of Jesus. About His childhood we have only the Birth Narratives of St Matthew and St Luke, and the very revealing story in the latter Gospel of Jesus' visit to Jerusalem at the age of twelve.

It reads like a mother's reminiscence. After fulfilling the customs of the festival, Mary and Joseph leave for Nazareth in the 'caravan' of friends and neighbours. When they encamp for the night they discover Jesus has been left behind. So they turn back. For three days they search for him, going over all the sights likely to interest a small boy—the shops, the parade grounds and the vast stables under the palace. Finally they go to the Temple. They find Jesus absorbed in talk with the Rabbis.

As any other parents would be, Joseph and Mary are relieved yet exasperated. They remonstrate with the boy and he replies: 'Did you not know that I had to be in my Father's house?' That phrase 'I had to be' is clear in the text. It shows that even as a boy of twelve Jesus was aware of a particular personal relationship with God. He used an expression never before used of the God of Israel. Then, says St Luke, Jesus went home with them and was 'subject unto them.'

1. The home of Jesus

Eighteen years pass before the next recorded event in the life of our Lord. What happened in that time? All the usual things that belong to youth—development of mind and body, learning a trade, learning to live with people and experiencing joys and sorrows.

In his home he would have received a religious upbringing in prayer and worship, in studying the Scriptures and taking part in the rituals of the home and the synagogue. The synagogue would have been his school as well as his church.

Mary and Joseph would have made their individual contributions to his development. We often think about his mother's share but Joseph's could have been just as important. The father was very much the head of the Jewish household. And Joseph's affection may have been reflected in the way in which Jesus used the word 'Father' about God without any hesitation. By contrast, it has been said that Martin Luther found it hard to do so because of the unkindness of his own father. That home at Nazareth was a school of life for Jesus.

2. The school of life

Is this true of the family today? All human institutions are undergoing stress and change and this includes the family. Its structure has changed. Father is no longer the sole breadwinner and consequent source of authority. But there is greater partnership and independence among members of the family. The material circumstances are greatly improved but the family is under pressure from inflation, housing shortage and social insecurity as well as from the effects of easier divorce, moral permissiveness and the decline in religious allegiance. Many of those who work among children in education, welfare and the area of juvenile delinquency seem to think that the family itself is in danger of disintegrating and the children are the most immediate casualties.

3. *What do children need?*

What do children really need from the home in the turmoil of modern life? As an indication one might quote the answers of some children who had been through the experience of broken homes, when asked what they liked and disliked most about parental behaviour. This was the substance of their replies:

Parental Virtues	Parental Vices
Truthfulness	Nagging
Honesty	Impatience
Fairplay	Lack of forgiveness
Courtesy	Affectionate displays in public
Quiet voices	Favouritism
Good cooking	Self-pity

There was no mention of generosity or comfortable homes. But behind the list lay a basic demand for a parent to be consistent, for parental love to give security and for it to have a value for the child whether he is successful or a failure—as did the father in the parable of the Prodigal Son. This is the home for which there can be no real substitute. It is one where a child finds values which will work when he goes out into the world—values of himself, of other and of God. It is the school of life or should be.

As Christians we must be concerned not simply with 'Christian family life' but with every home and its welfare in every aspect, moral, economic and social. We must be aware of any pressure which would reduce it to an impersonal and functional unit in social planning, the ultimate casualty of an irresponsible society.

We believe that the family was the setting in which the Son of God prepared for life. We believe that it is still the setting in which children should have the opportunity of becoming what they are above all else—the children of God their Father.

EPIPHANY

Christ at work

CARPENTER OF NAZARETH

The Jews and the Greeks had diametrically opposite views about manual labour. The Greeks associated it with slavery and so the free men despised it. The Hebrews held a high view of the dignity of labour. The accounts of the Creation depicted it as the work of God. Psalm 127.1 even spoke of God's co-operation with man in the building of a house. Many Proverbs warned against the sin of idleness. The Rabbis exhorted every man to learn a trade, as did St Paul who was himself a tentmaker. In 2 Thessalonians 3.10 he stated bluntly: 'If a man will not work, then let him not eat.'

So it was fitting that when the Messiah came, he should be a worker—unlike the founders of many other religions. In the teaching of Jesus there are many references to work and workers including, for example, agricultural labourers, builders and fishermen. Their work was an essential part of their life. It distinguished one man from another. But it was not the whole of his life. For what mattered was not only the work being done, but the person doing the work. And that statement is at the heart of the Christian understanding of the meaning of work in the modern world.

1. *A man and his work*

But the matter of work today challenges some of our traditional assumptions about it. We may be shirking the real issues if we talk about 'the dignity of labour' or 'every job being a vocation' or 'the state of life unto which it shall please God to call me'. Some jobs have as little 'dignity' as meaning for the people who have to do them, in an increasingly industrialised and complex mass-society. They would challenge any easy assumption that *laborare est orare*—that working and praying can be equated.

Work itself we take for granted, assuming that from one's teens to retirement, it will supply an essential part of one's *raison d'être*. The slumps of the 1930's saw millions out of work. Nowadays men fear redundancy. In the industrial world of tomorrow people and skills can be redundant. Are men without work to be men without purpose?

2. *What do people need?*

If we approach the problem of work not from the angle of its function in society but from the angle of the man engaged in it, we have to consider some of its implications for him as a person. For instance, how does he come into it—by accident or by design? The choice of a job or career matters to him but it matters also to the community, to a man's family and indeed to his church. And here the church must ask itself what it is doing to help its own young people in making this kind of decision and finding a real vocation. What are the criteria—pay, prospects, pension, time-off . . . or fulfilment of service?

Fulfilment is important. That might include some possibility of creative achievement either in the job itself or in the relationships in which it is done. All too often people find it difficult to see the significance of what they are doing in relation to the total effort of an enterprise and its part in the whole life of the community.

Relationships matter too. It used to be argued that there was such a creature as 'industrial man' who could be separated from the same man in his family or neighbourhood or church. But he is a person, to be treated as a person in every situation. He expects to be able to participate, therefore, in the making of decisions which affect his life. He does not want to be regarded as a mere unit, to be used for profit or power by anyone, whether employer or state or industrial organisation. The present demand for participation at every level of life of the community is a valid one and thoroughly Christian. So too is the expectation that this will be a responsible participation, giving as well as receiving.

3. The way ahead

The work situation has changed and will continue to do so. The 30-hour week is not far away. We shall have to ask ourselves how we will use the vastly increased leisure time not least in terms of service. If we believe that God is concerned with the whole of life, then that will include what we do with our leisure.

But what difference does being a Christian make to our work, let alone our leisure? Does it affect the quality of what we produce and of our relationships with those who work with us? Do we believe that the Gospel has any practical relevance to the work which takes up so large a part of our life?

And there is another side to that question. If our religion is to be seen as relevant to our work, then our work must be relevant to our religion. One could wish that more of the laity, if they are sensitive to what is happening in the realm of work in which they are engaged, would bring back into the Church their insights into the problems and developments. For if the Church is to be of service in the community it must be made aware of what is happening outside itself and the experience and the wisdom discoverable there. For the Holy Spirit does not confine his work to the four walls of the Church. He can be found in the laboratory, the classroom, the factory, the hospital, the bank, and at the kitchen sink too.

EPIPHANY

Christ in people

Albert Schweitzer said that he often found Jesus coming to meet him in the people to whom he ministered at his hospital in Lambarene. Are we aware that this can happen to us in the events of everyday life? Take, for instance, one's own diary and what happened in one week a few years ago.

1. *Sunday—a Baptism*

Steven was being baptised in a village church. The congregation included some of the villagers as well as the family and friends. It was a village which had been 'invaded' by a new housing estate. That can create problems. But the Vicar was a wise old priest who challenged the local congregation to welcome 'the stranger within the gates'. So the Church helped them to find a warm and understanding fellowship. This was a church being truly the Body of Christ.

2. *Monday—a prize giving*

Alfred had come to the C. of E. secondary-modern school resentfully. His two brothers had gone to Grammar Schools and then on to universities. Alfred had failed his 11-plus through idleness. He had been a bitter and difficult pupil. But the staff had persevered with him and won his confidence. So today he was being given his certificate with half-a-dozen O-level equivalents and could make up the ground to follow his brilliant brothers. His parents were deeply grateful to the school, and so was Alfred. Christ the teacher of his disciples—and they had been difficult pupils—had been reflected in the teachers at that school.

3. *Tuesday—a visit*

She was not far from death and she knew it. The parson was there to give her and her husband Holy Communion at home and he felt it a great privilege to do so. They had been married for thirty years. It had been for better, for worse, for richer, for poorer. They had been faithful to their mutual commitment and now their love was their strength when like Jesus in Gethsemane they received the cup in complete trust in God.

4. *Wednesday—a letter*

The parson knew it had been a poor sermon, preached on the subject of the woman who had touched the hem of Christ's garment, but ill-prepared. Yet here was a letter from a woman who had heard that sermon the night before she went into hospital for an operation. She wrote that she had been very worried. But just when she was being got ready for the operation there had suddenly come into her mind the thought of the woman who had touched Christs garment. 'I prayed for help and suddenly I was at peace. So thank you for that sermon'.

The parson felt himself humbled as well as grateful, for the fact that Christ had made something of his own poor effort. Once more Christ had turned the water of human effort into the good wine of the Gospel.

5. *Thursday—a memorial service*

The church was crowded with representatives of the life of that great city. But there were also six young men who represented the greatest service done by the deceased. He had been a magistrate. Often there had come before him some young man in trouble, with no family or friends to keep him from slipping deeper into the mire of crime. Time after time the magistrate had said: 'I'll look after him. He can come and live at my home for a while.' Some of these young men had let him down. But many others did not. He had not said: 'Somebody ought to do something about this case'. Instead he had accepted the responsibility himself. In his life he had shown the meaning of great words of the Gospel, like Salvation, Redemption and Reconciliation, not as theological doctrines but as Christ in action.

6. *Friday—learning to walk*

The parson went to hospital to visit a parishioner who had lost one leg in an accident. Two nurses were helping him to walk again with an artificial leg.

Later the parson left and walked back to his car. Suddenly it came to him—the realisation that he could walk easily and naturally without having to go through all his friend was facing. He felt ashamed that before he had arrived at the hospital he had been depressed by his personal and parochial problems.

Jesus had come to him and helped him to look at his life from the situation of another man's need.

7. *Saturday—nothing happened*

A service, meals, letters, accounts, interviews, telephone calls and a sermon to complete. The usual 'Parson's Saturday'. Nothing unusual except that he found that someone had left a newspaper on the prayer-desk in the church. Why? Or rather—Why not? Christians are bidden to pray for the world. The newspaper challenged one to be specific, to bring before God people bearing burdens of responsibility, the newly born, the newly married, the newly bereaved.

The newspaper was saying: 'This is the world for which Christ died, and he comes to meet us in it.'

EPIPHANY

Christ and happiness

1. *The Beatitudes, then and now*

Jesus said: Blessed are the poor in spirit, for theirs is the kingdom of heaven.

The world says: Blessed are the self-assertive, for theirs is the kingdom of power.

Jesus said: Blessed are they that mourn, for they shall be comforted.

The world says: Blessed are they that are sorry for themselves, for they shall be excused.

Jesus said: Blessed are the meek, for they shall inherit the earth.

The world says: Blessed are they that insist on their rights, for they shall get what they want.

Jesus said: Blessed are they that hunger and thirst after righteousness, for they shall be filled.

The world says: Blessed are they that could not care less about righteousness, for they shall never be called hypocrites.

Jesus said: Blessed are the merciful, for they shall obtain mercy.
The world says: Blessed are the merciless, for it's every man for himself.
us said: Blessed are the pure in heart, for they shall see God.
The world says: Blessed are the broadminded, for they shall see Jeslife.

2. An impossible ideal?

Those are two contrasting views of happiness. The word translated 'Blessed' in the Beatitudes means in the original: 'O, the happiness of . . .' So Jesus was not giving an idealistic picture of what might happen if people followed a certain line of conduct. He was stating facts, saying that happiness already belonged to certain attitudes towards life and these were the results of them.

All this would have seemed revolutionary to His contemporaries. Public opinion might sympathise with poverty, humility and mourning, but it took success and status to be the rewards of the good life and signs of the approval of Providence. People then as now might have agreed with the man who said that if he tried to run his business on the basis of the Beatitudes he would soon be bankrupt.

3. Does it work?

But do the world's standards bring real happiness? As set out above, they may seem in an extreme form but they are only the logical implications of contemporary values pressed upon us.

The first one assumes that self-assertion is essential. But we rarely ask which self we are asserting. It brings us power and status—a measure of our insecurity as well as of our pride.

The next reminds us how reluctant we are to accept responsibility even for ourselves. It reminds us of the boy in trouble who asked his father: 'What's wrong with me . . . heredity or environment?' We blame other people or our circumstances rather than ourselves. We feel that we would be happier and better people if we had a change—of job, perhaps even of husband or wife.

Then we are more concerned with our rights than with our responsibility. This is another side of our insecurity. We can seek to obtain our rights with total disregard for the effect of our actions on others.

We are hungry for our rights, but not for righteousness. But

Jesus saw this not negatively as something 'holier than thou'. He spoke of it as a warm and loving right relationship with God and therefore with one's fellow-men.

That would include showing mercy. This is not the condescending forgiveness of those who bury the hatchet but never forget where they have buried it. It is the readiness to share with others the forgiveness one has oneself received from God. But there can be no mercy where there is fear and insecurity.

Neither can there be a vision of God where there is no purity of heart. Purity is not a matter of attitudes to sex. It is more than sincerity, which can be the most dangerous of virtues. It is the wholeness of dedication to God, the true broadmindedness which looks on life and people in the context of God's love.

4. The choice

Which way lies happiness? If one wants pleasure and power, then Christ's Beatitudes are not the answer. The way of obedience to his Gospel means a cross as well as a crown, suffering as well as joy. This, as Jesus forecast, is to be expected. In the eyes of the world, he was a failure. They might acknowledge that he had not just taught the Beatitudes, he had lived them—and look where they had brought him!

They had brought him to the perfect service of God and Man, to be the supreme means of grace to humanity. He was able to offer the true and lasting happiness of fulfilment of man's real nature as the child of God, asking only the response of faith to the love of God. For happiness is not achievable as an end in itself. It is the by-product of living the life of Sonship

LENT

Christ and temptation

1. *Does it matter?*

The speaker was a regular churchgoer.

'Frankly, the temptations of Jesus in the wilderness have never meant much to me.' He said 'Even if he was tempted to turn stones into bread, or jump off the pinnacle of the Temple, or bow down before the Devil himself, what has that to do with Christianity?

What has it to do with me? I'm never likely to be tempted that way!'

A fair question worth thinking about as we begin our observance of Lent—what does the temptation mean to us in the twentieth century? But to answer it we still have to go back to see what it meant to Jesus.

2. Why the Wilderness?

If you stand at Jericho by the excavations of the ancient cities and gaze westward, you see the high grim scarp behind which lies the Wilderness of the Temptation. There Jesus went after his baptism in the Jordan at the hands of John. That in itself was surprising. One might have thought that with so much to do and so little time in which to do it, Jesus would have been anxious to start his mission immediately. Instead, he went away by himself for over a month to think and pray in solitude. There he worked out his priorities and his methods.

3. The first choice

Those were times of economic hardship and heavy taxation. Many were desperately poor. They would gladly follow anyone who provided them with food. To turn stones into bread—the flat round stones of the wilderness looked like home-made loaves— would bring a quick response. The very compassion of Jesus would impel him to adopt this policy. Surely, one might argue, when the physical needs were met they would be more ready to hear the Gospel? The suggestion would have a twentieth century ring about it. In the grim 1930's with slums and economic depression, many thought that if only we could have a true welfare state for all, people would be happier and better.

But Jesus knew the real answer, that man does not live only by 'bread' but by the truth of God. Of course Jesus was concerned about the basic needs of food, shelter and clothing and so must the Church be in every age. Christianity must demonstrate a total Gospel concerned with the whole human situation. But life means more than the circumstances of man's environment. It has to get down to the roots of man's failure to make the best use of that environment. Salvation is about the whole man in the whole world. The spiritual is as much part of that world as is the material.

26

4. *The second choice*

In his parables, especially in the one of the Sower, Jesus showed that he had no illusions about 'consumer-resistance' to the truth. So as he faced the future, he would see the possibility of shocking people into awareness of his message by miracles. This would meet a genuine want. The people longed for signs that God still cared and that God could still act. They would surely respond to miracles. But what would be the depth of that response? Later Jesus showed his answer to that question by deliberately avoiding publicity for his works of healing. He knew that the response would be superficial. For it was always easier to tempt God by demanding miracles than to live according to God's will.

5. *The third choice*

Then came the last choice, according to St Matthew's order. It raised the question of the use of power. Politically at that time Palestine, and for that matter the Roman Empire, was in the melting pot. A really effective rebellion could liberate Palestine and might even do more than that. History recorded how in Assyria, Babylon, Greece and even Rome, a single tribe had seized power and risen to dominate millions. It could happen again. So this was no mere exercise in wishful thinking. Moreover it was an alternative to the way of persecution and suffering which lay ahead for Jesus and for his Church. But Jesus rejected the way of force and compulsion. It was wrong to use evil methods to achieve right ends, however good the cause, however great the suffering it might avoid.

6. *Means and ends*

This is a question of paramount importance in the modern world although it is evaded wherever possible. Even in church affairs we are tempted to say, 'After all, it's for a good cause,' and to compromise over a matter of principle. We fear being criticised by the world for being narrow-minded when in fact it is the world which is being narrow-minded and refusing to face the wider implications of some line of action. Yet when we compromise we are, curiously enough, disappointing the world which unconsciously expects from us a positive witness which it cannot provide for itself.

So the temptations were ours as well as Christ's and they did not end in the Wilderness. They recurred in other forms. But he had established his priorities and his methods of fulfilling them in establishing the supreme 'good cause'—the Kingdom of God.

LENT

What price sin?

Sin is ridiculous. This was how many mediaeval sculptors depicted it. The roof-bosses at Southwark Cathedral, next to London Bridge, represent greed, lust and other sins by faces and actions which are absurdly sub-human. The artists were saying that sin occurs when man descends to something lower than his true nature as the child of God.

They faced the fact of sin. Nowadays the very word is dropping out of our vocabulary. We are willing to discuss morals, social responsibility and situation ethics. But sin is out of favour. That may be because it is a basically theological concept. For sin is something we do against God.

The idea of sin is also considered to be old-fashioned in the light of psychology. The Seven Deadly Sins have been explained away. Pride has become Self-Fulfilment. Anger is Stress. Avarice is Competitiveness. Envy is Insecurity arising from love-deprivation. Sloth is Inertia. Gluttony is due to defective metabolism. Lust is merely emotional response.

The Church also is accused of having encouraged people to be morbidly introspective with dangerous feelings of guilt about their natural instincts especially in respect of sex.

The uncomfortable truth, however, is this. Even if we have abandoned the idea of sin, we have not freed ourselves from the effects of what we must no longer call sin. They seem to be still with us.

1. *The Bible view*

The 66 books of the Bible are less inhibited about this matter than we are. The Old Testament reports the sin of Adam as disobedience and defines that of Cain as envy combined with irresponsibility. The early writers were well aware of the social consequences of personal behaviour and emphasised that sin caused the destruction of the community as well as the individual—a theme outstanding in the account of the wilderness and in the story of King David. They appreciated how these consequences could persist from one generation to the next. But Jeremiah and Ezekiel had to counter the habit of blaming present evils on the faults of ancestors and emphasise the responsibility of the individual for his own life.

The prophets stressed that, unlike the gods of other nations, Yahveh was a god of moral righteousness who would respond to true repentance. They showed him to be concerned with good and evil in the realm of international relations.

It is true that the later compilers of the Law tended to concentrate on ceremonial and ritual sins in their anxiety over the purity of the nation and of its worship. But at least they helped men to see that every detail of daily life could be the concern of God. We owe to the Psalms some of the deepest expressions of the problem of personal guilt and restoration. They describe sin in three aspects— as rebellion against God, as deliberate choice of the wrong direction of life, and as 'missing the mark' through weakness of character. As in Psalm 51, they plead that God will make man a clean heart and renew a right spirit within him.

2. What Jesus said

Our Lord brought to this age-long problem a two-fold solution. One was a new clarification of the nature of sin. The other was the power to deal with it. He saw the problem as concerned with the depth of man's personality rather than with externals of behaviour. At its worst, sin was the wilful rejection of truth and goodness. It was never simply a personal matter for it inevitably affected the lives of others. It had to be countered by positive goodness—the exorcising of the unclean spirit would otherwise merely leave room for more evil to enter. And the elimination of sin must be by the will of man, reaching out in repentance and faith to the forgiveness of God. Ultimately sin was conquered by the self-sacrifice of Jesus himself, bearing the sins of the world and reconciling man to God.

This was the victory which made freedom from sin potential for all men. St Paul experiences it as the fruit of being 'in Christ', when one has 'crucified the flesh' with Christ. St John writes of it as the life of freedom which comes from 'doing the truth', which Jesus had promised his disciples.

3. The way of freedom

Nowadays we search desperately for freedom but rarely in terms of freedom from sin. We live in a slavery to fear, to insecurity and to doubt. What the Gospel offers is a freedom which starts from honest awareness of our condition and of our own sinfulness. For a man sins when he looks on himself as the self-sufficient centre of his universe, when he treats people as things existing to serve him, and when he regards God as, for all practical purposes, dead. This is the deadly trinity of human perversity.

In Christ's parable, it was not the complacent Pharisee who would know the true happiness, but the Publican confessing himself to be a sinner. When we have the honesty to see sin as a reality, and to give up pretending that it does not exist or does not matter, then we can begin to hope for the Kingdom to be established in the hearts and wills of men.

LENT

Holy Villains

The idea that Jesus was interested only in good people is certainly not borne out by the Gospels. Quite a number of the 'heroes' of his parables are villains, rather than people of perfect character. But he did not describe them simply to criticise their behaviour, or with the spurious 'Isn't this shocking!' attitude of the scandal-monger. Instead Jesus simply singled out their behaviour to illustrate some great principle in the Kingdom, either of God's activity or of man's response.

1. The Bad Characters

Jesus usually simply recounted the behaviour of the bad characters. The Labourers in the Vineyard abused the messengers of God and slew His Son—and the audience got the point. The selfish and uncouth behaviour of the inconsiderate wedding guests spoke for itself, but it also typified the blindness of those who refused the invitation to the Kingdom which Christ himself was conveying. In both parables the villains represented the very people to whom he was addressing his teaching. They were not third parties being criticised at a safe distance.

Occasionally the conventional roles of 'Baddie' and 'Goodie' would be reversed, to the amazement of the hearers. They were as shocked as was the lawyer to find the Samaritan made a hero, and the Priest and Levite under criticism. Similarly, in the parable of the Prodigal Son, they were not disturbed by the happy ending of the reconciliation of the father with his penitent son. But they were affronted by the treatment given in the story to the Elder Brother. After all, he had behaved himself according to the strict letter of filial piety and family obligation as understood and practised by the Jews themselves. But the last act of this domestic drama exposed him as childishly resentful of the fuss being made over his brother, just as were the Jews at the idea that God's love for all mankind might possibly put other nations on the same footing as themselves.

No one minds a sermon which underlines the wickedness of the world or criticises the behaviour of other people. But being forced to recognise themselves depicted as villains was not likely to make Christ's audiences welcome his teaching. As a congregation may sometimes complain about its preacher: 'His sermons are much too personal. Why doesn't he stick to the Gospel?'

2. *Values upset*

It must have been even more disturbing when Jesus seemed to treat even the character of God with apparent levity. He was speaking about the need for persistence in prayer. Then, as now, people were inclined to expect instant results when they prayed and to be disappointed when nothing happened. Then they tended to blame God or, in a better mood, to get anxious about their own sins which might be a barrier between themselves and their heavenly Father.

Jesus took an entirely different line. He told them that the trouble lay in their lack of persistence. They must keep on praying until they received some response. To illustrate this, he told them the story of the Widow who nagged at the unjust judge 'who feared neither God nor man' (St Luke 18.1–5), until he gave her revenge on her adversary. In the same Gospel (11.5–10) we have another parable on the same theme which tells us to go on praying with as much persistence as the man who wanted to borrow three loaves and got his neighbour out of bed through his importunity (literally, 'bare-facedness'). It would have been startling to hear God compared, even implicitly, to an unjust judge and a reluctant neighbour. But the message would have gone home. And this method was along the lines of paradox which Jesus used so frequently in his teaching. They could say of him as they said later of his disciples that he had 'turned the world upside down'. That is exactly what he did to many conventional ideas of right and wrong and of God and goodness.

3. *New villains and new heroes*

In those days Christ disturbed the conventional ideas of the religious. He does the same today. But his Gospel also disturbs some of the conventional ideas of the non-religious. They belong to people who are dangerously conformist in their notions of values and relationships and their superficial humanism. Theirs is their new Establishment which is rigidly anti-everything concerned with truth and beauty and goodness. The secularist society produces its own mythology of Celebrity-Gods, its own Commandments of social acceptability, its own Gospel of optimism to cover up its spiritual poverty. Its heroes need to be exposed to honest scrutiny, even if as a consequence they are blown away by gusts of laughter.

The true heroes remain. One thinks of people like Albert Schweitzer and Pope John among the men, and Gladys Aylward among the women. They have not been the heroes of the power-cult but servants of humanity. As such they have won respect. Their lives with all their strengths and weaknesses have been like acted parables demonstrating, as did the parables of Jesus, the principles of the Kingdom of God.

LENT

What is purity?

When Jesus said 'Blessed are the pure', his audience approved. When he added, 'in heart', they were uneasy. They thought they knew all about purity, just as we think today. But in fact Jesus' new concept of purity was as disturbing to their idea of it as it is to ours.

The Jews thought of purity in three contexts. First, there was the realm of religion and morals. In the heathen world there was little connection between public religion and private morals. Gods and goddesses were thought of as living on a moral plane actually lower than that which men might expect of each other. Worship in the temples had little bearing on personal conduct. In

Palestine, the nature cults of the 'high places' had a highly sexual content against which Judaism had to battle for centuries. Judaism on the other hand set a high value on purity in sexual matters and in family life.

Purity of race was also very important to the Jews. After the return from Exile in the 5th century, the religious leaders strongly opposed mixed marriages with 'the people of the land'. Circumcision and the Sabbath and food taboos were important elements in the defence against the loss of identity of the race.

In the day to day life of the people these elements were very significant. So too was ritual cleanness including the avoidance of defilement by contact with blood. In the Good Samaritan story, the Priest and the Levite were from this point of view only doing their duty by avoiding a defiling contact which would have prevented their fulfilling their ritual obligations. Impurity happened to a man from outside.

1. *The teaching of Jesus*

In St Mark's Gospel, 7.15, we have the sharpest statement of Jesus' revolutionary principle of purity. He said that nothing from outside really defiled a man for defilement came from inside. This would have been seen as upsetting the whole purpose of the religious laws relating to purity. His apparent neglect of Sabbath restrictions, his lack of concern about washing his hands before a meal—behaviour of this kind would have been seized upon by his enemies as evidence of his destructive attitude to the Law itself. To them this was blasphemy for the Law was the Will of God.

But Christ's attitude was not merely one of opposition to established custom. He substituted for the negative view of purity as the exclusion of evil, the positive view of it as a continuing attitude of the whole personality, in other words, the 'heart' of a man. This concept had been foreshadowed in Psalm 51.10 and Ezekiel 18.31, for example, in prayers for a clean heart and a right spirit. But Jesus expanded and deepened it in the emphasis on inwardness which characterised his approach to the whole problem of personal morality.

The Sermon on the Mount must have shocked those who believed they knew the meaning of the moral life. They regarded murder and adultery as evil deeds. But Jesus condemned the contempt for one's fellow man which could result in the act of murder. He spoke about adultery not only as a bodily act, but as something of which a man was already guilty when he lusted after a woman. He put the focus of attention not on conduct but on the motives which lay behind it. And there purity was of paramount importance, so much so that it would be rewarded with the vision of God.

2. *The difficult definition*

So, clearly, purity is the opposite of evil and it is the attitude of the whole personality. But can one go further in defining it positively without emphasizing the negative aspect, of what purity is not? One has to recognise also that since motive is important, behaviour which might be described as 'pure' in one situation might not be so in another. At least it is clear that purity is not confined to problems of sex. On that, however, St Paul touched in 1 Corinthians 3.16, writing: 'You are the temple of God, the Spirit dwells in you, the temple is holy'. In Philippians 4.8, he stressed that purity meant the concentration of the mind on the good, on everything that is honest. just, lovely and of good report. So purity is not to be thought of as negative or static, but as dynamic. In other words it is the personality in active relationship with the self, with others and with God.

3. *Purity and reverence*

The outstanding characteristic of this relationship can be summed up in one word—reverence. Reverence is the recognition of holiness and of sacred character, whether it is of one's body or the body of another person. It means treating someone else as the creation of God. It is an awareness of the essential holiness of what God has created.

This is why in the Beatitude, Jesus said that the pure in heart 'shall see God'—not only in the beatific vision of the life eternal after death, but here and now. This was how Christ saw God. His purity of heart looked past the outward circumstances of the publican and the prostitute to their longing for God which was the ground of their redemption. He called his disciples to a holiness far exceeding the righteousness of the Pharisees in terms not of externals of conduct but of the inward disposition of the personality, the awareness of God in life.

This is the purity for which humanity is searching in the moral confusion of our time. It is the reverence which puts sex in its rightful context of love. It helps us to achieve meaningful relationships with others because we start with a high value of them. It shows man, as he searches for identity and asks 'Who am I?', that he is not a thing but a person, holy to God. This is his true humanity which Christ redeemed for every one of us.

LENT

The Lord's Prayer—in reverse

THE DIFFERENT PRAYER

The disciples said to Jesus, 'Lord, teach us to pray'. They were already accustomed to praying. This was an important part of their religious life. Yet they were acutely aware that his praying was different from theirs. It was the expression of a continuing relationship with God. So they were asking him to teach them how to experience that relationship as well as to express it in words.

In reply Jesus gave them what we know as The Lord's Prayer. He began where they were already, with God, but with a difference, as 'Our Father'. Then he spoke of the being of God, His holiness and His will. Only then did Jesus bring in a petition, for bread as the basic necessity of life. Immediately he moved on to things spiritual, to God's forgiveness associated with man's forgiveness of his fellows. Next came a prayer for help in temptation and finally for deliverance not from poverty or danger, but from evil.

1. *The Prayer today*

Jesus could start from where the disciples were already, from a situation of belief in God. Where could we start today? There are many who want to believe and to pray, although they might not describe their deep-felt need in those words. Their feelings are like letters sent without an address on the envelope, even without any clear idea of what the letters are meant to express. If they start anywhere it would be with the last clause of the Lord's Prayer and they might have to work back to the beginning.

Praying it backwards

So I begin with 'Deliver us from evil' where many people are already, worried by the evils of our time, its cruelty and corruption, where goodness and faithfulness, purity and kindness seem to be at a discount. Deliver us from evil, indeed, but does that mean only some divine intervention to eliminate the destructive forces of our time? But I am compelled to admit that inside me is the little world

35

—the microcosm—which both reflects and contributes to the large world outside. So I have to learn to pray: 'Deliver me from the evil within myself.'

That evil within me is most powerful in certain recurrent situations where 'temptation' is not a general danger but specific. Each man has his own vulnerability. So 'Lead us not into temptation' becomes personal. I face the fact that I am my own worst enemy and I need help. So I ask God to make me aware when temptation comes and to be with me in dealing with it.

2. *Forgiveness comes next*

I look at my life and I know that I need a wholeness of the soul, integration instead of the disintegration through conflicting desires. I cannot achieve liberation from the past by my own efforts. Psycho-analysis may reveal me to myself. But it cannot give me the power and the will to become a different kind of person. I need absolution and forgiveness which can help me to forgive even myself.

But how can that forgiveness be effective if I am not prepared to forgive others? That is not just a religious obligation, it is a fact of my life as a 'social being', to use Aristotle's phrase. And I must admit that the offences others commit against me are trifling compared with those I commit against them and against God. So, God forgive me and help me to forgive others.

3. *And so to bread*

It seems a long jump from praying about relationships to praying about food. But it reminds me that perhaps I take for granted the essentials and only value them when I am in danger of losing them. Health and food and shelter and work—they, like relationships are gifts for which I must exercise a responsible stewardship to God.

4. *And in the end—to God*

I should now be able to face the movement in thought from petition about myself to something wider. I have to live in a world which can conquer space but not the space within men's minds. I must pray that instead of human plans and policies, there must come about the acceptance of a higher will for mankind by which national and international efforts can be assessed and guide. But if I pray that God's will should be done in the world, in all honesty I must pledge myself to live by that same will. God's rule must be allowed to come into my life as well as into the councils of nations. To do that I must 'hallow His name'. That means taking God into account in my own life. For without the holiness of God, there can be no holiness and no wholeness for the individual or for the church.

Our God is 'in heaven', and heaven lies about us here as in eternity. And it is the last phrase which tells us where we come home, to the God who is our Father. That is where we end—where Jesus began.

LENT

Commitment

The item 'Apologies for absence' can give a somewhat depressing start to a committee meeting. Sometimes the excuses offered are reasonable. Sometimes they betray that the absentees just cannot be bothered to attend. Then they remind one of our Lord's comments on the human tendency to break a pledge when to keep it means effort and sacrifice.

St Luke's Gospel has two significant passages on this theme. In the 9th chapter, Christ speaks of those who aspire to discipleship but give first place to other interests. 'No man having put his hand to the plough and looking back is fit for the Kingdom of God', he said. He put God's claim even above the family duties which the Jews regarded as of paramount importance. This was one of our Lord's hard sayings but it is at the heart of Christian vocation.

In the 14th chapter, we find the same point made in the parable of the wedding feast. The guests have already accepted the first invitation. Then on the actual day they 'give back word'—to use a North of England expression—for reasons which seemed superficially adequate. Two plead business and one pleads the obligations of matrimony. None attaches any weight either to the convenience of his host or to his own personal commitment.

1. *My word is my bond*

There is a twentieth century flavour to those excuses. The idea that one's word is one's bond is becoming a rarity. Instead, we must have contracts. Even then we cannot be sure that the small print will not provide a way of escape from that impressive 'guarantee'. Much of the machinery of the Law has to be taken up with this problem. Behind it lies our reluctance to keep a promise.

37

The Church is not unaffected by this tendency. All churches are concerned about withdrawals from the ministry and about lay reluctance to fulfil obligations of leadership. The Religious Orders are also being affected. In missionary service, life-time commitment is giving way to short-term contracts. Often the explanations given are reasonable and understandable. Nevertheless, there are situations where clearly little priority has been given to the obligation to the Church itself. Perhaps the basic problem is one of confusion over the meaning of vocation and of over-riding concern for one's personal happiness.

2. The pledge in human relations

Jesus put the problem in the context of a wedding. We can see it in the setting of Christian marriage today. In the Prayer Book service, the bride and groom promise 'to love, comfort, honour and keep, in sickness and health, forsaking all other . . . to have and to hold from this day forward, for better, for worse, for richer, for poorer . . . to love and to cherish till death do us part . . . .'

These are tremendous promises and they are quite exceptional in contemporary relationships. There are other instances of pledge-giving in the life of the Church. In the setting of Holy Communion, the Sovereign takes solemn oaths at the Coronation. So do the deacon, the priest and the bishop at ordination and consecration. So too do the godparents when standing sponsor for the child at Holy Baptism.

3. Keeping the pledge

There is a clear thread running through all these services. On the one hand, the Church is asking ordinary human beings to make promises which are demanding and life-long. These pledges might seem hopelessly beyond the attainment of everyday humanity.

But they are not impossible. They have been kept and are being kept. That is because in response to the covenant made on the human side, there is grace on the Godward side. St Paul puts the promise of Christ in these words: 'My grace is sufficient for you' (2 Corinthians 12.9) and at the end of his letter to the Philippians, he writes: 'I can do all things through Christ who strengthens me.' He had experienced the way in which God enables men to give their word and keep it, to find fulfilment in God's service, and to achieve what the New Testament calls significantly 'The crown of life.'

38

4. *The pledge of the Church*

We try to discover what is the Church's calling and function in the modern world, mainly in terms of activity and service. But Evelyn Underhill once wrote that we are always conjugating the wrong verbs—to do, to have ... but not the verb 'to be'. Perhaps we should think afresh about the being of the Church, and ask questions about its convictions and commitment, its devotion and its faith, its obedience to the guidance of the Holy Spirit.

The witness of the Church in this generation depends on its being composed of people committed to truth and willing to accept and fulfil the obligations of that commitment. There could be a spiritual renewal and a spiritual revolution if we would put into action those familiar words:

> O Jesus, I have promised
> To serve thee to the end ...

PASSIONTIDE

The gifts of the Passion

In the last week of his earthly life, Jesus who gave so much, gladly received seven gifts from other people. They make a strange catalogue—a donkey, a box of ointment, a room, a shoulder, a request, a drink and a tomb. Each played an important part in the Drama of the Passion.

The donkey came first, used by Jesus on his Palm Sunday entry into Jerusalem as a kind of 'visual aid'. It reminded people that, as the prophet Zechariah had foretold, their true king would come in humility and not in pomp. It was a kind of acted parable which, like all Christ's parables, sifted the audience into the perceptive and the unperceiving.

Then came the box of scented ointment, given by Mary anointing him for his Passion. She was somehow aware that what was developing could end only in death. As he went his way in loneliness, she gave him the gift of sensitive understanding.

The upper room came next. Jesus needed somewhere to have a last meal of fellowship with his disciples. There he instituted the sacrament of Holy Communion which would sustain them through the terrible events to follow. That room saw also the unforgettable demonstration of true ministry when the Master washed the feet of each disciple.

1. *The gifts of Good Friday*

Tradition suggests that the man who gave Jesus his shoulder later became a Christian. When Jesus faltered under the weight of the cross, the soldiers compelled a bystander, Simon of Cyrene, to walk close up behind Jesus and share the burden.

The next gift was equally unexpected. It was a word of encouragement from a thief dying on a cross by the side of Jesus. He could rise above pain, with sudden insight to see in his fellow-sufferer one who could save with a power beyond death itself. He asked only for remembrance.

As he was dying, Jesus received another gift. It was a drink, part of a soldier's ration. It was given by a man who might have seemed hardened to suffering. Yet when he watched the Galilean, he was strangely moved to do something to ease his agony.

The last gift was a tomb, given by one who had not dared to acknowledge publicly his admiration for Jesus and to risk incurring criticism. That tomb was to be the scene of the final victory over death. Like all the other gifts of the Passion, it was accepted and transformed in the service of Christ.

2. *The seven gifts today*

Each of these gifts played its part in the Drama of the Passion. And they embody principles of timeless relevance. The donkey was the sign of humility but also of greatness, as Christ used it. Wherever we are privileged to encounter someone of truly great character, we meet humility also.

The gift of the box of ointment may seen to be outside our experience. Yet what Christ asks of us is that however preoccupied we may be with our own problems, we should be sensitive to the suffering of others.

The upper room is every church and every dwelling where Christ is at home. He is the unseen guest, communicating himself. And the quality of service we give to each other in the family or the church and in the world is our memorial of the washing of the feet.

The gifts of Good Friday may seem remote from our style of living. But the dying thief asks us if we have the faith in Christ which stands up to the test of suffering and even when facing death. For as with this stranger, what matters is our belief in Christ.

When he received the soldier's wine, our Lord's own experience was illustrating his own teaching. He had said that the criterion of Judgement would be what we had done consciously or unconsciously to others 'Inasmuch as you have done this . . .'

And finally, the tomb, from a man who had been reluctant to identify himself with Jesus. Does the old hymn: 'Stand up for Jesus' belong to a by-gone age or is there a place for positive self-identification with Jesus today? The question can come to us unexpectedly as it did to St Peter in the person of a serving-maid. Sometimes it stands out clearly when decisions are being made. Perhaps we have been too ready to compromise over issues of right and wrong in order to be accepted by the world. We have been satisfied to maintain a silent 'Christian presence'. We have been afraid of being labelled 'difficult', 'un-cooperative' or 'prejudiced'. We are willing to provide a tomb to bury Jesus, but not to acknowledge him as the Living Lord. Joseph of Arimathea is the patron saint of lost opportunities and nervously self-protective Christianity.

The six other gifts were in varying degrees gifts of identification with the person and mission of Jesus, and the last was of belated commitment. In every Christian's life there are times when Christ's mission asks of him or her a gift—of humble witness, of sensitivity to need, of fellowship, of practical support, of faith in darkness, of sympathy or even of something we have been keeping for ourselves as Joseph did. When we respond, then, as happened in the Passion, the gift and the giver can be transformed.

PASSIONTIDE

Pilate's questions

Some of the most important questions Jesus had to face were asked on Good Friday by one man . . . Pontius Pilate. His first may have been put with scornful amusement. 'Are you the King of the Jews?' A mere Galilean carpenter! Jesus replied: 'My kingdom is not of this world . . . everyone that is of the truth hears my voice.' The whole statement seems to have made Pilate realise that Christ's power was of an utterly different character from that which he usually associated with kingship. Then he seized on the word 'truth'. 'What is truth?' he asked, in the manner of one sceptical of the claims to possess it made by religious and political propagandists.

Instinctively aware of the integrity and innocence of Jesus, Pilate addressed his next question to the mob: 'Which will you have set free, Jesus or Barrabas?' Surely their common sense would lead them to prefer the guiltless Nazarene to the convicted bandit. They chose Barrabas.

Then Pilate floundered. Instead of using his authority to make the decision himself, he demanded: 'What shall I do with Jesus?' The response was 'Crucify him!'. He tried again to make the mob face facts, saying 'What evil has he done?' The answer was an even louder shout for the death penalty. Pilate gave in. In a feeble attempt to clear himself of blame, he washed his hands before the crowd.

The day drew to its close but not before Pilate had asked his last question. The friends of Jesus came seeking the governor's permission to remove and bury the body of their Lord. St Mark's Gospel records that Pilate asked if the Nazarene had indeed died and required certification from the centurion in charge of the crucifixion. He wanted to make sure that the whole affair was over. But it had really only just begun.

1. *Pilate's questions are ours*

Throughout the centuries Pontius Pilate has been condemned for his cowardice and his readiness to let self-interest over-ride his plain duty to release an obviously innocent man. But if we try to put ourselves in his place we might understand how his problem was really one which faces many of us in our own life-situations. His questions reflect those which arise in the mind of people in every age, including our own.

The kingship of Jesus, for example, is crucial for Christianity. We have to ask ourselves if we believe—and behave—as though Jesus is the lord of all life, risen and existing today. Or do we give lip-service to this doctrine while in fact we act as though Jesus is but a glorious example and his teaching an out-dated idealism. Again, if his power is not of this world, we have to ask if the Church ought to be concerned with its political and social power and its prestige in the national and international scene.

Jesus said that everyone that is of the truth hears and obeys his voice. And Pilate asked what truth is. Like Pilate, we are sceptical about truth, subject as we know ourselves to be to political and ideological propaganda. We are tempted to conclude that there is no such thing as truth, no standard by which such claims can be verified. Our greatest credence is given to what we call 'scientific truth' which demands 'practical' evidence and distrusts faith. Yet one can question whether this kind of approach gives the whole truth about life. Pilate could not recognise that the real truth about the meaning and purpose of life stood before him, not as a set of abstract propositions but as a way of life embodied in the person of Christ.

2. The questions to the crowd

Pilate tested the opinion of what the 17th century dramatist, Massinger, called 'the many-headed monster, the giddy multitude'. They chose Barabbas. This was not the first or the last time in history that the mob has preferred evil to good, when it is made to feel insecure by demagogues appealing to the emotions under the guise of appealing to reason. Truth and justice are swept aside. And the situation can rarely be saved except by a minority who dare to be different. We have to ask ourselves what witness we are prepared to give in a situation where we honestly believe the majority opinion to be wrong on some vitally important question of morals or political or social action—or if we take refuge in silence. It is easy to despise the multitude, but Jesus 'was moved with compassion towards them, because they were as sheep not having a shepherd' (St Mark 6.34). Compassion may mean witness as well as service.

3. The last question

Pilate's final question is the most important one for the Church as for the world. He asked, 'Is he dead?'. If so, then Jesus deceived himself as well as others. As St Paul put it, 'If Christ is not risen, then our preaching is vain and our faith is vain.' (I Cor. 15.14). But the Apostle knew from his own experience and that of the other Apostles, that the most signal proof of the Resurrection was not the empty tomb but the transformed lives of those who experienced the Risen Lord. And it is still so. The Church is and must be the Church of the Resurrection to give the world the true answer to its ultimate questions about death, and about life.

The Marks of Christ

The world asks 'What is the difference, between the Church and other 'do-good' organisations, between the Christian and any non-Christian who tries to lead a decent life?' A fair question. It is put by people who genuinely, and perhaps hopefully, would wish to find in Christianity a way of life with a meaning and value greater than that of any of the panaceas offered in the world today. On the first Easter night Christ gave the answer to that question.

1. *He did four things*

St John's 20th chapter describes how the ten disciples met in fear and confusion—ten, because Judas was dead and Thomas was absent. They feared the hostility of the Roman and Jewish authorities. They were ashamed of their desertion of their Master in his hour of need. They were disturbed by the reports that Mary Magdalene had seen Jesus and that Peter and John had found the tomb empty. They hoped—but did not dare to hope.

Then suddenly he was with them. His first greeting was 'Shalom' —a word of peace and forgiveness.

He showed them his hands and the wound in his side. These were the marks by which they could identify him unerringly—no phantom, no figment of the imagination but the Crucified himself.

Again he said to them: 'Peace be unto you' as if reiterating the word of forgiveness, and he went on . . . 'As my Father has sent me, even so send I you.' So they became Apostles, literally 'those who are sent', with a new commission like that which Jesus himself had received from God.

His last act was to give them the Holy Spirit with a new authority in respect of the forgiveness of sins.

2. *The four acts in the Church*

On that first Easter night Jesus gave his disciples forgiveness for their betrayal of him. Every church and every congregation needs his same gifts. It is dangerously easy for us to tolerate division among ourselves, turning a blind eye to evil in our corporate lives. The world rejects advice on reconciliation when it is given by any Church which is obviously itself unreconciled and without penitence. We must pray: 'Lord, convert your Church, beginning with me!'

3. *The mark of suffering*

The second act revealed the marks of suffering. Pastor Niemoller said 'If the Church is not suffering, it must ask itself if it is truly the Church.' The Church is called upon to suffer today wherever Christians are persecuted for their religion; for political reasons behind the Iron Curtain, in areas of Asia where adherents of other religions are hostile to Christian evangelism, where the Church tries to witness in defence of the value of men irrespective of race or tribe or colour. In the West the persecution is often more subtle and less obvious. It takes place when the Church tries to take a stand on moral values to asks searching questions about materialistic ideas of progress or about group-conflicts in the community. But only rarely does any Church seem willing to witness to the point of suffering on these issues. Instead we seem content to be by-passed. When this is true of Christians corporately, it means that Christians individually rarely feel any obligation to stand up and be counted on some moral issue, as Christ suffered for the sake of truth and compassion.

4. *Apostolic means 'Sent'*

The third act was the commissioning. The disciples were being sent, with a new mission and responsibility. It might have sounded absurd, this mission to a hostile Jewish and Gentile world by a mere handful of people, to 'go, teach, heal, baptise, make disciples of all nations.' The sheer effrontery of it! But they felt themselves to be men under obedience, men supported by the sufficient grace of God. And after constant persecutions, despite inner failures, within three centuries Christianity had become the religion of the empire.

Does the Church and the Christian have that same sense of being 'sent' today? The contrary sometimes seems evident. We are self-conscious about the role of the Church in the welfare state and uncertain about the uniqueness of Christ and his Gospel. The general weakening of a sense of obedience has its effect upon vocations to the ministry and to religious orders. Yet, as the Epistle to the Hebrews insists. Christ saved mankind by his obedience and this obedience must be at the heart of Christian mission. It involves every one of us. As the Willingen International Missionary Conference decided in 1952—'There is no participation in Christ without participation in his mission to the world.'

5. *Spiritual Authority*

The fourth act of Christ made clear one essential characteristic of Apostolic mission, that it is spiritual. There are other elements in it of course—healing and reconciliation, witness to truth and to human values, the care of the sick and broken, the service of the community, for example. But Christ's words about sin and forgiveness are very significant today. We are inclined to deal with problems as though they were merely weaknesses, the product of bad environments and pressures, or minor accidents in the course of automatic human progress. We try every means of assistance—except the grace of God, brought to bear on men's lives when they have realistically faced the fact of their own responsibility and acknowledged their fault. Then they can be reconciled to themselves, to others and to God.

6. *When the four acts take place in us today*

The result is for us, as it was for the Apostles, a deep happiness. 'Then were they glad when they saw the Lord'. Where the Church or the Christian reaches out in faith to the Risen Christ and accepts his forgiveness, receives his Spirit and is willing to obey his command, the consequence can only be a new joy which is itself infectious.

We started with the question 'What is the difference . . .?' On that first Easter the answer became apparent in the lives of the Apostles, the night that the Church was born.

EASTER

The patron saint of doubt

It is an oddity of Christian history that one indication of the reality of Christ's resurrection should come from the refusal of one man to believe in it.

Thomas had been absent on the first Easter night. He then refused to concede that Jesus had appeared to the others. He insisted that unless he saw the prints of the nails in the hands of Jesus and touched the wound in his side he would not believe. He would not accept the evidence of the amazing transformation in the disciples. Perhaps the very vehemence of his language concealed his longing to see the Lord.

A week later, his demand was met. Jesus came and offered his body to be touched. Thomas could only say 'My Lord and my God. Then Jesus said: 'Because you have seen me, you have believed. Blessed are those who have not seen and yet have believed.'

Jesus did not criticise Thomas for his doubt. He had no illusions about the problem of faith. But he gave his blessing to the millions who through the centuries have been willing to take him on trust.

1. *Why believe?*

The importance of the question was evident from the earliest days of the Christian mission. St Paul had to face it at Corinth where many of the recent converts were in doubt about the centre of the Christian faith, the resurrection of Christ. In the 15th chapter of his first Epistle and elsewhere when he is dealing with this subject, the Apostle based his case upon three arguments. One was the evidence of those who had actually seen the risen Lord—including himself, last of all. Another was the appeal to Scripture which figured so prominently in the Apostolic preaching of the early Church of which we have an example at Pentecost. The third was the appeal to reason, which he made in 1 Cor. 15.35–49. In addition, St Paul stressed that being 'in Christ' was the experience of the risen Lord open to all Christians even if they have not seen his bodily presence.

2. *The three streams of faith*

Is St Paul's approach still valid? Four hundred years ago Richard Hooker, the theologian, dared to suggest that in searching for truth one should bring together three converging streams—Scripture, Tradition and Reason.

First Scripture—of course we begin with the Bible as the record of God's dealings with men and of their varying response to Him through centuries of history. In all honesty we must not be afraid to subject this library of 66 books to searching enquiry as to authenticity and authorship. We have nothing to lose. Truth is more important than convention. We do not regard anything as essential to salvation which is not in accord with Scripture as a means by which God conveyed his Word. But we do not make the mistake of claiming that the Bible has explicity 'all the answers' to contemporary questions, many of which simply have no analogies in the life-situation of the Biblical writings.

47

We turn to the stream of Tradition. By this we are thinking of the living experience of the whole Church through twenty centuries. This is the Church where the Holy Spirit has been at work leading towards the truth. His leadership has often been resisted. Christians have settled for doctrines which they have been reluctant to re-examine later because they were important to a fixed view of authority and function. Tradition has sometimes had assigned to it an unwarrantable infallibility and treated as superior to the Bible or to reason. But the three sources hang together and are mutually interdependent, as they have been in the living development of the Church itself.

And reason is no less important than the other two. Today Christians have to get away from the insecurity which prevents their venturing out into the world. There the Holy Spirit is active as he is inside the Church. We assume that reason can guide in personal life and relationships. It is basic to moral responsibility. It is part of the basis of spiritual growth. To have faith is not to deny reason or to feel threatened by science. It is to accept the world as the realm of God's activity and be willing to learn from the insight and exploration there.

3. No simple Gospel

All this is of course very demanding. It is far easier to choose one of the three streams of truth and reject the others. One can worship the Bible with near-idolatry, or close one's mind to anything except 'what the Church teaches' or live by a superficial materialism which one claims as 'scientific' and based on reason. But Christianity dares to expect one to attempt to hold all three in a creative tension —and to do so, in St Paul's words, 'in Christ'. For when one studies his teaching, one is suddenly aware that this is exactly how Jesus presented the faith. He accepted the Scriptures and illuminated them, looking for the principles behind the laws, in the light of living experience and using God-given intelligence to work out their implications. And he never apologised for the demands he made on people's intelligence. He never offered that fiction of the sentimentalists—a 'Simple Gospel'.

For if real doubt is never simple, neither is the truth which meets the need that lies behind it and enables the doubter to say 'My Lord and my God.'

EASTER

The last enemy

A tourist looked at a 'memento mori' in Salisbury Cathedral. It was a full scale representation of a human skeleton on top of a mediaeval tomb. 'What a morbid lot they were!' he remarked.

A widow was talking about her bereavement. 'My friends expected me to get over it quickly, like measles. They would not realise that it was like an amputation.'

1. *Facing death*

That mediaeval tomb belongs to an age when men lived close to death. The average expectation of life was not much more than thirty years. Infant mortality was high. Disease, pestilence and war were constant threats. Consequently the fact of death figured prominently in the art, literature and religious discussion of the time.

Today many of those threats have passed. Infant mortality is greatly reduced. At least in western society the average expectation of life is up into the 70's. But death is still the near neighbour from death on the roads to death from the stress diseases of modern life. Perhaps the main difference is that the subject itself is almost taboo. Evelyn Waugh's *The Loved One* and Jessica Mitford's *The American Way of Death* have exposed the commercialism and hypocrisy accompanying the attempt to pretend that death has not happened, and to gloss over its effects on the bereaved. We are embarrassed by grief and criticise the Victorians for their demonstrativeness in mourning. Our new beatitude is 'Blessed are they that do not mourn'. But grief denied outlet, endured in loneliness and without hope, can destroy personality and we are slowly realising this.

2. *The Christian attitude to death*

Opinion polls show that a very high proportion of members of churches have ideas about death which are not very different from those held by non-Christians. This is so despite the fact that belief in the Resurrection is one of the central tenets of the Christian faith, stated in the Creeds and prominent in many hymns.

It might be argued that this is a good thing. Men have lost their fear of death as an event leading to the pains of judgement and the torments of hell for all but the saintly. Another gain has been that men have tended to look on this life as of value in itself and have recognised the need to improve conditions of human life here and now. They have been less inclined to put up with injustice and lack of social progress, in the expectation of rewards in the hereafter. The keys to the kingdom hereafter have become less important than the key to happiness here.

3. What has been lost

On the other side, we have lost a sense of accountability and meaning. If death is the end, then men can feel that they can get away with anything in this life without having to face any judgement on their conduct. Another loss is that there is no answer to the problems of injustice, waste of life and bereavement. Suffering seems pointless and we are easily inclined to think that selfishness and evil are triumphant. This point of view may seem logical to atheists. But it cannot be so to those who believe in God. For the chief reason for belief in life beyond death lies not in human need—although this is almost an universal instinct—but in the nature of God. Because God is God, death cannot be the end.

4. The teaching of Christ

This fact is reflected in the teaching as well as the life of Christ. He did not speculate about death and the after-life. His parable about Dives and Lazarus used a traditional Jewish picture of the future to make a particular point about the reversal of human values in God's assessment and indeed about the importance of compassion in present life. He exposed the futility of the Sadducean standard joke about the resurrection, which they did not believe in. He simply stated that in the life to come marriage as a social institution would not exist. At certain key points he was quite definite in his teaching on this subject. To his disciples, he said that in his Father's house there were many 'dwelling-places' and that he was going there to prepare a place for them. They must trust him.

To the thief dying on the cross by his side, Jesus said: 'Today you shall be with me in Paradise'. Again he uses a conventional term. But what is important is that Jesus speaks of 'You' and 'I', implying that in whatever stage of existence lies ahead, personality and relationships continue.

To the bereaved Martha he made his most significant pronouncement: 'I am the resurrection and the life'. This sums up for all of us the personal implication of what was the Christ's Resurrection on Easter Day. For, as St Paul and St John saw, the eternal life lived in Christ begins here and now, transcends death and continues beyond it. Christ put his teaching into action in the continuing fellowship with him which his disciples experienced after his Resurrection. As St Paul wrote—'Death is swallowed up in Victory.'

5. What does this mean for us?

If death is a beginning as well as an end, I must accept it and not try to pretend it does not happen. I must prepare for it just as I would prepare to emigrate to another country or start another job. It is idle for me to speculate on the kind of life I shall experience after death. It is sufficient for me to know that it will be a life. And life means personality, relationships, development and freedom, greater than I can know here on earth. I know that all I shall be able to take with me will be myself—my record, my memories, my failures and achievements. When I think about judgement I remember St Paul's words towards the end of his chapter on Love . . . 'then I shall know even as I am known'. That might be the worst judgement of all for it will be utterly revealing. But I remember that my Judge is also my Saviour, that God is my Father as well as Almighty and All-knowing. In that hope for the future, I find new hope for the present.

ASCENSION

The Church of the Ascension

We start with a comment and a question from two children. The comment came from a young confirmation candidate. Talking about the period between the Ascension and Whitsun he remarked: 'It must have been like when you first ride a bike on your own.'

The question was that of a child who was looking at a stained-glass window depicting Christ in glory. He asked his mother: 'Mummy, what does Jesus *do* all day?'

1. Learning by stages

Jesus was a master teacher. He never disclosed to people more of the truth than he thought they were capable of receiving at the time. His training of the disciples proceeded by stages which merged into each other. In the early days they had been called simply to be his companions. After many months of watching and listening, they faced the test question at Caesarea Philippi which asked what they thought of him. Then, assured of his Messiahship, they could be taught deeper things about its meaning. They were also ready to be sent out in pairs to do what today we might call pre-evangelism, learning to make contact with people and to prepare the way for the Master.

Next came the third stage, of the Passion with all its intense demands upon their faith and its exposure of their own need.

Easter began a period of companionship with Jesus deeper than anything they had known before. It is difficult to assess from the Gospels all that happened at this time. The Fourth Gospel ends with a meal on the lakeside during which Jesus spoke of the future martyrdom of Peter. Acts 1.3 speaks of a period of forty days when Jesus talked to the disciples of 'the things pertaining to the Kingdom of God'. Perhaps he shared with them deeper theological teaching, not least about himself, which the experience of Easter had prepared them to receive. It seems to have been a time when he was with them only intermittently, as if getting them ready for doing without his visible presence.

2. *The time of departure*

Then came the last conversation, which was once more on the subject of the future. The disciples were still thinking of this in terms of the restoration of the messianic kingdom. But Jesus was teaching them about an entirely new stage when the Spirit would have come upon them and they would be witnessing to him throughout the world. And on this note, he left them, in a manner which, like the account of the Transfiguration, is described in colourful imagery.

Once more the disciples went down from a mountain top to a valley beneath, and so back to Jerusalem. But this time it was not to be engaged in works of healing or mission. They had to pray and wait. They had to learn to do without the visible presence of their Lord, knowing that as he prayed for them on earth, he would continue to pray for them now.

3. *Jesus the High Priest*

The belief that Jesus was praying for them became a growing conviction in the early Church. It is expressed most fully in the

Epistle to the Hebrews. The theme of the High Priesthood of Jesus runs through the whole letter, particularly in such passages as 9.24: 'Christ is entered into heaven itself, now to appear in the presence of God for us.'

In the 12th chapter, Christians are counselled to run with patience the race that is set before them, 'looking unto Jesus the author and finisher of our faith ... who is set down at the right hand of God.' The anonymous author would not have interpreted the statement in the Apostles' Creed—'And sitteth on the right hand of God the Father Almighty'—in terms of a static role. He would have thought of it in relation to the activity of our Lord, caring for his Church, in a close and continuing relation with it. This is how the Christians thought of the Ascension, not as the end of a relationship but as the beginning of a new one with Christ the Mediator and Redeemer. This, to answer the child's question, is what 'Jesus does all day'.

4. *At which stage are we?*

The commemoration of the Ascension has suffered from two main problems. One, at a somewhat pedestrian level, is the simple fact that its observance comes in the mid-week when people are too busy with other things. The other arises from our pre-occupation with the mode of the Ascension rather than its meaning. We associate it with something which we have abandoned, the three-tier concept of the world with Hell beneath us, Earth on the middle stratum, and Heaven above. The New Testament simply describes the Ascension in the picture-language of its own time. It is not the language that matters so much as the idea and the experience which it conveys.

The meaning which it had for the Apostles is still relevant to the Church of our own time. The question, however, is whether we have reached the stage at which its significance can be appreciated.

In our spiritual growth we can stop short at various levels. The first stage of uncommitted Christianity is an easy one. We too can enjoy the watching and the companionship. To get to the next stage, we have to face up to the question of Caesarea Philippi and accept Christ as Saviour as well as Friend. We find, as the disciples did, that this involves us in mission and sharing in the outreach of the Church.

Then comes a time of the Passion. Unpopularity, ridicule, hostility, betrayal and outright failure come to test our faith and our loyalty and we can be found wanting. It is hard for us to see that Calvary may be the only way of saving the Church as well as the world.

If, by the grace of God, we survive, then we can come to be the Church of the Resurrection. We live with the presence of the Risen Lord and learn the deep truths of the Gospel about life and death, about time and eternity. Then we walk by faith and not by sight, knowing that Christ is praying for us. We can be ready to be filled with the Spirit and commissioned for our Apostolate.

5. *The Question of the Ascension*

The real question of the Ascension is therefore not about the way in which it took place, but about our own readiness to receive it. We have to ask ourselves what stage we have reached—and perhaps remained at for many years—in what should be a spiritual growing, of ourselves as Christians, or of the church and congregation to which we belong.

This is a question of importance to all Christians. It is of particular relevance to those of us who have been called to the ordained ministry. To us, as to the disciples, Jesus says: 'You have not chosen me, but I have chosen you and ordained you, that you should go forth and bring forth fruit, and that your fruit should remain.' Ordination is not a static condition of status or authority, but the beginning of development, as priests, prophets and pastors. When that process of growing is difficult and even painful, we have the assurance which those first Christians shared, of the promise of the Ascended Lord, in the last words of St Matthews's Gospel: 'Lo, I am with you always, even unto the end of the world.'

WHITSUNTIDE

The Church on fire

The name 'Whit Sunday' is derived from the fact that the newly baptised came to church in white robes, on this day commemorating the confirmation by the Spirit at Jerusalem. This was the day of Pentecost, meaning fifty days after the Passover. At the Temple Sanctuary the first-fruits of the harvest were presented in the form of two wheaten loaves. It was a joyous festival attracting thousands of pilgrims to the city.

1. The Spirit comes

Ten days earlier Jesus had left the disciples, telling them to wait for 'My Father's promise'. He had spoken of Someone coming to be with them. In the interim, they had done nothing except bring in Matthias to fill the gap left by Judas because they believed they were to be the new messianic community representing the twelve tribes in the New Israel.

Suddenly it happened. The account in Acts uses vivid picture language of the sound of wind, lights like flames and a torrent of words. The twelve felt driven out to face the crowds they had previously feared. Then Peter preached the first sermon of the Apostolic Church which embodies what was to be the main theme of its testimony at the first stage of its mission.

He challenged his audience to recognise that this was the baptism of the spirit foretold by the prophet Joel when all who invoked the name of the Lord would be saved. He proclaimed that Jesus of Nazareth, of whose death they were all aware, was the promised Messiah. He had been raised from the dead, even though he had been crucified.

The response of the audience was simple and direct. 'What are we to do?' they asked. Peter's reply was equally direct. They should repent and be baptised for the forgiveness of their sins and they would receive the gift of the Holy Spirit. Hundreds of them did so. But the new converts were not left without help. They came together frequently to receive instruction, to pray and to 'break bread' together in common meals and in Communion. They lived communally sharing their possessions. They opened their homes to each other. They went to the Temple together daily. So the early Church went into action.

2. What does it mean now?

This second chapter of Acts reads like an idyllic success story of direct challenge winning immediate response, remote from our contemporary experience. In all honesty, Acts goes on to record the other sides of the Church's life including the grim example of hypocrisy in the case of Ananias and Sapphira, and the arguments about the rations for widows. But the Pentecost story has its own challenge including, in the opinion of some, a rebuke to modern Christians for their reluctance to expect the phenomena of spiritual gifts such as healing and speaking with tongues. The Pentecostal movements are certainly making us think about this.

But St Peter's sermon asks us if we give due place to the proclamation of the Risen Christ and to the call to repentance. It asked for faith and it offered forgiveness, as had the preaching of John the Baptist. People took it personally and asked what the Gospel required of them as individuals. The Baptist did not hesitate to make a specific requirement in terms of each person's situation. So did Jesus with the rich young ruler. Wherever evangelism is effective, the general call is translated, perhaps with the help of counsellors, in terms of the individual's situation, to meet his need.

3. A Church in Mission

Those Apostles believe that people needed repentance and forgiveness, and a spiritually and physically sustaining fellowship. Instead, it sometimes appears as though all Christians offer their fellows is a lukewarm invitation to join a club for the mutually and socially compatible if they have nothing better to do. One may wonder if the world sees the average Christian's reluctance to evangelize not as broadminded tolerance but as an almost insulting lack of concern for the outsider's needs. A recent convert to a 'fringe religion' commented: 'I don't know whether their doctrines are silly or not, but at least they were concerned about me and wanted me.'

What the Apostles had to share was a joyous personal experience of what Christ had done for them and what the Spirit was doing for them. They found no pleasure in regarding their generation as crooked and evil. They cared about people and wanted them to know the joy of the Resurrection and the power of the new life. This was a positive approach and hundreds welcomed it. They accepted the fact that to enter this experience meant costly and searching repentance, and a complete change of outlook on life. It was no optional extra for them, neither was it for the Apostles.

We have to ask ourselves about this especially when we are concerned about the weakness of contemporary evangelism. Can this be due to preoccupation with our own problems, to lack of faith in Christ, to indifference to the spiritual, as well as the social and moral, problems of others? If someone were to want to become a Christian and were to ask 'What should I do?', how would we answer him . . . and why? Evangelism is not only a proclamation of doctrine. It is a communication of life.

If the question makes us uneasy, perhaps like the disciples we should take time off from our ecclesiastical and religious busy-ness and pray for the Holy Spirit to show us the answer. And it might start with a call to repentance leading to new joy in the Lord.

WHITSUNTIDE

The Sacraments down to earth

KEEP RELIGION SPIRITUAL?

Archbishop William Temple said that Christianity is the most materialistic of all religions. This is exactly what some people complain about. Perhaps understandably, they would prefer to see it as a way of life concerned with higher thought and aesthetic values. They value meditation and devotion but dislike being expected to become involved in the corporate activities of the Church at the level of the local congregation. They abstain from what they consider to be the mere routines of worship and sacraments. They are suspicious of any Christian involvement in social problems. They see their religion as essentially spiritual and personal.

People with this outlook are but part of a great number including those who hold to the old idea that 'one can be a Christian without going to Church' and the recent spread of what one might call 'Christianity without the Church'.

1. *Is membership necessary?*

This is the real question which lies behind these three attitudes. To answer it we have to start with Christianity in the teaching of Jesus and in the practice of his followers. It is clear that the New Testament knows nothing of a Christianity of isolated individualism. Jesus called men to follow him and become members of his fellowship. Saul of Tarsus was converted as an individual. But he took steps as soon as possible to link up with the very church he had persecuted. He came to know better than anyone else the failures and frailties of the new congregations. Yet he constantly stressed the importance of responsible and participating membership. 'We have this treasure in earthen vessels,' he wrote, 'that the excellency of the power may be of God and not of us'. The very 'earthiness' of the Church was for him a demonstration of what we know as the sacramental principle which is of crucial importance to Christianity.

2. *The sacramental principle*

This is, quite simply, the fact that God works through things, through events and through people. The Gospel begins with the Incarnation whereby God becomes Man. It ends with the Death and Resurrection whereby God redeems and liberates Man.

Between the two, there is a constant instrumentality by which people and things become media of God's grace. Christ uses everyday objects to accomplish miracles. Indeed, he speaks of himself in terms of things used in the home, as the Bread, the Gate, the Way, the Light, etc. Through a towel and water he reveals the meaning of ministry. Through bread and wine he gives himself to his disciples.

3. *Does this matter?*

Jesus demonstrated that the material, itself belonging to God, can be the means of conveying the spiritual and of responding to God. The Father works this way because He knows what man needs.

It seems unrealistic therefore for one to claim a superiority of status or character enabling one to be able to do without the sacraments as a means of grace. After all this claim was not made by the saints who should have been able to be spiritual isolationists, if anyone could do so. When people assert that they do not need the sacraments of Baptism or Eucharist, or an ordained ministry or even the Bible, it is not impossible that they are claiming a spiritual aristocracy which does not harmonise with the humility of the Gospel. That is not to say that the sacraments cannot be in danger of over-familiarity or an almost mechanical use. As the Corinthians had to learn, the abuse of the sacraments can be spiritually dangerous.

But they are not only individual activities. They are also extensions of the principle of coherence, of Christ uniting his Church as described in Colossians 2.19. Seen from this angle what a sacrament does for one personally has to be set in the context of its corporate significance. When I 'make by Communion', my initial mood or my final awareness of grace may be inadequate and even disappointing. But I have been doing something of wider importance, to the church as the body of Christ in that place.

Of course there have been and will continue to be arguments about the extent to which the effectiveness of a sacrament depends on the degree of faith in the response of the participant. In this connection we may argue whether infant baptism precludes the need for a conscious self-commitment in 'believer's baptism' later. We will disagree about the desirability of baptising children when there is little likelihood of their being sustained by a Christian family.

These aspects are important. But even more so is the recognition that these are means of grace, and grace is the gift of God's loving kindness and wisdom. They are to be received not as a right but as a privilege, not with pride but with humility, with penitence but also with joy. For they are the gifts of the Father, given to his children within the Family of faith. And the Family of the Church for all its faults, is meant to be yet another means of grace. For it was Christ's intention and Christ's invention, not man's. And after all as Archbishop Temple described it, the Church is the only society in the world which exists for the sake of those who do not belong to it.

WHITSUNTIDE

The heart of worship

When Jesus went to the Temple he did not gaze at the architecture or the ceremonies. He watched the people. He looked beyond the worship to the thoughts and motives of the worshippers.

His disciples were impressed by the lavish giving of wealthy contributors to the Temple chest. Jesus drew their attention to the widow giving all she possessed in a mere farthing. In proportion to her income, her contribution far exceeded that of the wealthy.

On another occasion, Jesus was critical of the ostentatiously pious who offered prayer where they could be seen and made a display of their fasting. And there may have been a human story behind his stern injunction about reconciliation before daring to worship. One can imagine his noticing a man coming to make his gift at the altar, whose very expression indicated hostility towards another worshipper. Jesus said: 'Leave your gift before the altar'. Go away and first be reconciled, then come and offer the gift.'

1. The question of motive

Christ was making his disciples consider what motives may lie behind any act of worship and indeed what really constituted worship itself.

Worship has to be looked at from three angles, the Godward, the Corporate and the Manward. The Godward seems to have had rather more attention in the past than it does today. The great cathedrals remind us of those who gave of their substance, their craft and their artistry. One thinks of the constant offering of prayer in churches and homes throughout the centuries and in the religious orders. All this belonged to the *Opus Dei*, the 'work' offered to the glory of God and offered for the sake of the world.

2. Corporate worship

Today we tend to concentrate on the corporate aspect. We think of worship as the exercise of the Church as the Body of Christ in which the whole 'laos' of the people of God play their part. St Paul had to teach this to the church at Corinth as almost a new experience, in which every individual made his offering complementing the contribution of others. This is part of the modern liturgical movement. Every church is moving from 'concerto' worship where the priest or minister is the soloist and the congregation is the supporting accompaniment, to what we might call the 'symphonic'.

But the achievement of corporate worship is not an end in itself. We have to ask what it is doing to make us one body *in Christ* and not merely one body, and whether it sends us out to the world in mission.

We can drift into a 'lowest common multiple' form of worship which makes no demand on anyone, is emotionally satisfying and morally anaesthetising. But worship is meant to be more than comfortably corporate. It should bring us to penitence and prayer and thanksgiving, illuminate understanding of ourselves and of the world, and above all help us to the most important meeting of all—the communion with God.

3. Personal worship

Jesus himself used and taught the 'inner chamber' worship of God in personal prayer. And this is something which we have to learn to offer both in the context of corporate worship and in our own private lives. The two are more closely related than we may sometimes realise. When we worship along with others, the experience should be demanding something of us, as well as affecting us, as individuals. It should be also 'edifying' us—in the literal meaning of the word, giving us the materials for building a Temple within our own private lives.

We have to recognise also that personal worship is something not easily achieved. It demands concentration to overcome distractions from outside, and barriers from inside, in our anxiety and worries and fears. Our prayers can become superficial. Our motive can be merely that of a desire to escape from the pressures of life.

What matters most is whether the purpose of our personal worship is the true one, that of seeking communion with God. That involves the whole personality, of mind and emotion and will. It also asks that we should be prepared to accept the consequences. In Isaiah 6, the prophet was aware of God's holiness and of his own unholiness. Then he was cleansed as if by fire. He felt compelled to offer God service which sent him out to his fellowmen. He had come into the Temple at a time of national crisis following the death of the King. He found himself changed by the power of God and caught up in the Kingdom of God.

4. *The Risk*

This is the risk to which we expose ourselves when we let our worship become truly personal and a real meeting with God. For it can be a revelation of truth, about ourselves and about the whole of life. It can be a vision of God which cleanses and demands of us a new obedience even while it fills us with new purpose.

Or it can be none of these things—no sense of God's presence, no answer to prayer, no power to lift us above the distractions whirling about in our minds, no illumination of our immediate problem. Yet to worship in this darkness of the soul can be, from the manward side, the highest offering of all and God's silence can be the chastisement and testing by a loving Father of those whom He loves. For the aim and purpose of worship is after all in Jesus's words: 'Thy will be done.'

WHITSUNTIDE

Trouble in Church

The situation at All Saints is critical and a deputation has gone to see the Bishop. For some time there have been serious conflicts between three groups. One supports the first Vicar. Another favours the policy of a priest who was temporarily in charge of the parish. A third is demanding an entirely different policy of a kind associated with the name of another Bishop.

It is rumoured that the church is still further divided over a scandal concerning a prominent member of the congregation. He is alleged to be living with his step-mother.

Two members of the church have recently appeared in the Law Courts as complainant and defendant in a bitterly contested action over property.

Church services have been disrupted by arguments over the status and functions of various participants. At the parish breakfast after Holy Communion, instead of sitting together in fellowship, various 'cliques' have refused to share the common meal and have sat militantly apart.

Church collections have dropped. There has been no contribution to missionary work for some time.

It is understood that on his last visit, the Bishop, who was himself the first vicar of the parish, had a very rough reception. Some parishioners questioned his episcopal status. Others maintained that he was receiving too large a salary. Quite a number resented what they considered to be his 'narrow-minded' demand for a high moral standard of Christian conduct. He was told to recognise that whatever might be the practice at other churches, All Saints was different and the congregation had the right to set its own standards. They were, after all, citizens of one of the most famous and cultured cities in the world.

1. The Church at Corinth

The above report is simply a translation into contemporary terms of the situation to which St Paul was addressing himself in his letters to the Corinthians. Yet although the Apostle was well aware of the position, he dared to start by addressing the Corinthians as 'called to be saints'! Most of us might have been tempted to wash our hands of the matter and abandon the congregation to its fate. But Paul showed his greatness in the way he dealt with the situation. It provoked him not to anger but to superb statements of the essentials of the Gospel, on the subject of the Resurrection, for example, and in the passage on love which is among the religious and literary treasures of the whole world.

The reason was that he cared—both for the whole church which he saw as a strategic salient of the Kingdom of God, and especially for the committed minority that was the real heart of the mission in Corinth. The tensions and problems were serious enough, but the apostle recognised that they were very largely due to the fact that the members were Corinthians. In other words, they had brought their world in with them. They did not want to change. They did not want to accept the moral implications of being Christians.

2. *Scandal in the Church*

Every church has its scandals. They are rarely as sensational as those to which St Paul refers. But they are no less serious when they are the scandals of non-commitment, of the superficial membership which believes nothing, gives nothing and refuses to let religion make any difference to life. The tragedy for such people is that when they face a personal crisis, the hollowness of their religion is exposed. The tragedy for Christianity is that the world takes these people as being representative of the Church and condemns it accordingly.

3. *Detachment and Involvement*

The old phrase 'to be in the world but not of it' sums up the age-long problem facing us all. We are called to accept our involvement in the world because it is God's creation and the object of God's love. On the other hand, the Way, as Jesus demonstrated it, must also be the one of detachment from the false values and the obsessions of our human environment. Time after time the dilemma presents itself, not least in the realm of morals, as was particularly evident at Corinth.

St Paul set before his readers a high standard of discipline affecting their relationships within the church, in home and family life and their witness to the world. They were reluctant to accept it, and so are we. The Prayer Book rubric would debar from Holy Communion any 'who have done wrong to their neighbours by word or deed, or betwixt whom malice and hatred reign'. If any clergyman or minister of a church in this western society were to try to implement that discipline, he would soon be in trouble!

Is this because the world of Corinth still dominates life within the Church of Corinth?

The Apostle's reply was to remind them that they were called not to be spectators but to be Saints—with all that this involved in terms of faith and fellowship, in quality of corporate and personal life. And he addressed this call especially to the minority in this apparently hopeless situation. They were the ones ready to share in his own experience of suffering for the Gospel to which he refers in 2 Cor. 11. They were, as they always are, the remnant which God can and does use for the renewal of the Church and the redemption of the world.

WHITSUNTIDE

Listen to the Spirit

It was a conference with a difference. It had no agenda, only a text and four questions. The text came from the last book of the Bible, the Book of Revelation. This begins with a kind of spiritual balance sheet for each of the Seven Churches of Asia. Each analysis concludes with the admonition: 'Hear what the Spirit is saying to the Churches!' This was the text taken by this group of young men and women from a number of adjacent parishes as their overall theme for thinking and praying together.

1. *What is happening?*

They began by asking what was really happening in their local churches, behind the impressive list of services and meetings on the cover of the church magazine, the financial statements and the reports of organisations. It was not difficult to find evidence of the non-event and the mixture-as-before attitude which blocked initiative and impeded growth. It was similarly possible to look back on something which had taken an immense amount of effort and had nothing to show for it, save that it had involved a number of people in doing something together.

Then one of them asked if they ought not to recognise worship itself as a 'happening' in the life of the churches. After all, he pointed out, this is what makes the first impact on the newcomer and its depth and quality should have some effect on the lives of those who have participated in it. So they began to ask what happened in their worship—from the godward and the manward side.

2. *What is the Church for?*

When considering happenings in terms of growth and worship, the group found themselves doing so in terms of their value to people. So they were led to ask what the Church itself was for. Now one can define the functions of the Church in terms of worship, witness and work and these categories broadly hold good. But their application changes. In the past the Church pioneered in education and welfare, to an extent often forgotten now that these functions have been taken over by the State. Of course in all three respects, there are continuing and permanent elements but it is nevertheless justifiable to ask what should be the Church's worship and witness and work *now*. The writer of Revelation said to each Church: 'Hear what the Spirit is saying!' God's purpose for the Church can require new responses in new situations. It is God, not the Church, who knows what is its vocation.

3. *What do people need?*

The other side of the Church's vocation is that of meeting basic human needs. The group at the conference emphasized that 'need' is not the same as 'want'. People may want the wrong things from religion and the Church may be too concerned to meet popular demands to meet real needs.

So what do people need? It is essentially to find meaning and purpose in life, to be loved and to have the freedom and opportunity and help to fulfil their true natures. But they also need to give as well as to receive, to love as well as to be loved, to be encouraged and even challenged to aim high in quality of life and service. These were the needs which Jesus met as he offered men the Gospel of forgiveness and of grace. Of course the Church must be concerned with the needs of men for freedom and education and work and community, and its concern must be evident in action not in pious resolutions at conferences.

And as with these young people at this conference, we have to think about this question in its personal context. We have to ask what we believe to be our personal needs and how they are met in our own Christian experience. We have to ask also what are the needs of people in our own immediate context. Otherwise, like

Dives, we may well discuss the problems of the poor in Palestine while the pauper lies neglected at our door.

4. *How can we meet those needs by God's help?*

The last question reminds us of the way Jesus challenged the disciples at the feeding of the five thousand. The disciples had to provide the loaves. Then Jesus made the miracle.

We can easily fall into replying: 'Charity begins at home. We must first repair the church roof. We are so few and so poor and so old. What can we do in the face of such vast problems?'

We have to start with what we have and where we are, identifying the particular need. For instance, the massive movement of population which presents some of the greatest problems to the churches also affords opportunities of meeting need, of welcoming the rootless stranger and helping to give the new community a caring nucleus. Another avenue of service is that of encouraging the young people of the churches to find vocations where personal ministry is particularly important as, for example, in education, medical or social welfare, the police or probation service, to name but a few.

And in all this we do not offer a ministry of compassion in isolation but in partnership with many others, Christian and non-Christian alike.

Four questions, then, to the Church are perhaps best answered in the words of William Carey inscribed on the lectern in Westminster Abbey given in memory of this great Baptist missionary. He wrote over 150 years ago:

> Attempt great things for God.
> Expect great things from God.

WHITSUNTIDE

The test question

This is the age of questions. Our forefathers would have been amazed at the range of questions put to people today in census forms, Gallup polls, and market research enquiries. We are accustomed to being asked for opinions and information, even about intimate personal relationships. But very rarely are we asked basic questions about the meaning and purpose of our own lives. Yet this was the kind of question which Jesus put to people when he wanted them to face up to reality.

1. *What do people say?*

When about half-way through his ministry, Jesus withdrew with his disciples for a brief rest, to Caesarea Philippi, about 25 miles north of the Lake of Galilee. There, almost casually, he asked his friends what people were saying about him. It seems a curiously self-conscious question, almost out of character.

The disciples told him that people were saying that he was John the Baptist, or Elijah or Jeremiah or one of the other prophets. The answer was significant. It reminds us how much in the prophetic tradition was the teaching and mission of Jesus. They too had been not fore-tellers of the future, but 'forth-tellers' of the mind of God. As they had done, Jesus preached to the poor. Like them, he stood apart from the 'establishment', both political and religious. So many had seen in him the renewal of the prophetic revelation of God for which they had been hoping.

All this lay behind the disciples' reply. But Jesus made no comment on it.

2. *What do you say?*

Suddenly Jesus turned the searchlight of enquiry upon the disciples themselves. He asked them what they thought of him. It had been easy enough to report other people's opinions, as it always is. But to give their own opinion was quite another matter.

Their minds must have raced back through the past months to what had first drawn them to him. Then there were the miracles, the teaching, the insight, the authority, Jesus at prayer . . . and most of all the personality with which they had been in daily encounter.

Then speaking for them all, Peter said: 'You are the Messiah, the Son of God.'

We are so accustomed to this acknowledgement that it is hard for us to appreciate its full meaning at the time. It was an immense leap of faith and insight to accept Jesus in this way, to recognise in the Carpenter of Nazareth no less a person than God's Messiah. To the ordinary Jew, it would have been blasphemy. To the convinced disciples, it was a statement of fact.

From that moment a new stage in the training of the disciples began. Jesus could now give them teaching of greater depth than before, particularly in respect of the suffering which lay ahead. At first, Peter, like the others, was reluctant to face this. He had to be sternly rebuked for attempting to divert Jesus from his path. But they learned to trust him and to go on with him to the end where there would be the ultimate answer to all questions.

3. Public Opinion

The two questions recur throughout Christian history. Christians have always preferred the first to the second, not least in our own generation. At times we seem to be almost neurotically anxious about 'the image' of the Church, as if obsessed about success and failure and desperately wanting to be loved—although Jesus warned against this in St Luke 6.26.

But Jesus did not ask 'What do people say about *us*?' He asked what they said about himself and what the disciples said too. The question comes back to the Church. Whom do we say that Jesus is? We do not answer that question by proffering our creeds or our liturgies, for the importance of the question lies in the word 'is'. It asks if we really believe in the Jesus of the present tense, the Risen Lord who is the Head of his Church, whose Gospel is the divine word relevant even to this space-age. If so, then like the disciples we go forward in faith. If not . . .

4. Personal Opinion

It is easy to castigate the Church for lack of faith. But Christ's second question is inescapably addressed to the individual Christian too. Peter and the disciples answered after thinking over past experience and came to the only possible conclusion.

We have to think over our own discipleship and the ways in which Jesus has made himself known to us—in the Bible and the sacraments, in the fellowship of the Church and in the experience which others have shared with us. He has been meeting us in people and in situations. He has met us in answered prayer, but also in prayer to which there seemed to be no answer. Yet many of us will have no clear record of personal spiritual experience to quote. But what matters is that like the young man cured of blindness we should be able to say: 'One thing I know. I was blind. Now I can see.' Somewhere in our lives we have glimpsed the way, the truth and the life. And our own lives will be the real answer to the question 'Whom do you say that I am?'

WHITSUNTIDE

The Church and money

'The Church is here to save souls, not to balance budgets.'
'The clergy are always begging for money for something.'
'What I do with my money is my own affair. It has nothing to do with my religion'.

Those three remarks are often heard, even on the lips of Christians. True or false, they are part of the continuing debate about the place of money in religion.

The debate was going on in New Testament times. Jesus himself was concerned not so much with money itself as with its significance. Many of his parables were about it, as in the instances of the Lost Coin, the Buried Treasure and the Unfaithful Steward. Challenged by his enemies over the payment of taxes to Rome, he cut to the root of the one question by asking another about the meaning of the inscription on a Roman coin and established the principle of rendering to God what was His. The worship of money he condemned as nothing less than idolatry. To Jesus, money was not an end in itself but only a means. Moreover, a man's attitude to money could be an important indication of his priorities.

1. *Money in the Early Church*

Money figures prominently in the life of the first Christians. At first at Jerusalem they practised communalism, pooling capital and income and depending on a common fund. But they had their problems. There was controversy over the allowances to widows. Ananias and Sapphira provided the classic example of the contributor who wants more prestige than he deserves. The financial problems of the early Church are not uncommon among us today!

St James' Epistle sternly condemns a church which gave special favour to the wealthy at the expense of humbler members. St Paul had to argue about the right of a full-time ministry to adequate maintenance. He also expected each of the churches he founded to do something which seems a curious reversal of modern missionary policy—to contribute to the Mother Church at Jerusalem in a time of need. This was an important means of promoting mutual responsibility and inter-dependence.

2. *The meaning of Stewardship*

In recent years there have been interesting developments in Christian understanding of the meaning of money. Stewardship campaigns have helped people to realise that money is not primarily a possession but something of which one is steward and for which one must feel accountable. It is linked with the stewardship of time and talents.

Moreover, we have come to see that giving is not to be activated by occasional emotional response to charitable appeal. It must be thought about, prayed about and pledged at the maximum level one can afford and with fully responsible awareness of the need to be met. Stewardship becomes an inescapable obligation of membership.

But there is something more. Giving has to be seen as the response to need—not only the need of the recipient, but, even more important, the personal need of the giver to give.

3. *Priorities in giving*

All this may be accepted as a general principle within the life of the Church. But what weight does it carry when we move out into the world?

The Gospels suggest that our attitude to money is indicative of our priorities. So we might learn something about ourselves from the proportions of our income spent on self-indulgence or on charity, or from our honesty in filling out our tax returns. If as Christians we recognise that the only morally justifiable ways of receiving money are by wages, by services rendered, by goods supplied, or by gift—then how do we justify taking other people's money in gambling?

The same questions about priorities apply in the wider community. The pursuit of extra profit can cause widespread distress through redundancies. The battle for money by one section of the community can cause hardship to millions of other people.

We have to think about our priorities as nations. Our colossal expenditure on pet food, for example, makes our much-publicised contribution to disaster areas look absurdly small. We realise that we are citizens of one world. But we must ask if we are going to help the under-privileged only out of our superfluity or by voluntarily accepting a reduction of our standard of living to be able to help realistically.

Faced with a question about money, Jesus asked for what the Authorised Version calls 'a penny' and spoke about its inscription. Our present day penny bears the Sovereign's head and the inscription includes four letters which describe the Sovereign as D.G.—

by the Grace of God, and F.D.—Defender of the Faith. In a sense those two theological statements point us to the heart of our whole stewardship of life as well as of what we possess. To live by the grace of God and to defend the faith are the vocation of every Christian who seeks to 'Render to God what belongs to God.'

WHITSUNTIDE

Voluntary service

When I was Vicar of Leeds I put the same question to three successive Lord Mayors of that great City. At the end of his year of office I asked if during his twelve months as Lord Mayor he had discovered anything important about the City which he had not known before.

Each gave me the same answer. He said that he had never realised just how much the life of the city depended on the voluntary service of organisations and individuals. One of them added his opinion that the welfare state in general would grind to a halt without it. Another remarked how encouraged he had been by the number of young people in schools already involving themselves in voluntary service. 'This is a real training in citizenship', he said.

1. Service and discipleship

The term 'voluntary service' as such does not occur in the Bible. But its implications are illuminated by many sayings of Jesus. One might have assumed that he would have given it unqualified approval. But, as in so much of his other ethical teaching, our Lord posed questions about motivation. In the Sermon on the Mount he asked what reward one could expect when one loved only those who loved oneself, or did good only to those who returned good. The ostentatious almsgivers, he said, had received their reward in self-satisfaction and in the admiration of others. So they could not expect any further bonus from God.

A cynic once remarked that one of the greatest pleasures in life is to do good secretly and have it discovered publicly. We all know that an appeal for some good cause which publishes lists of subscribers and the amounts given, is more likely to succeed than one which omits to do so. We say that this is only human nature, to like being thanked and appreciated. But if this is really our motive, then we can hardly claim to be acting with true altruism or with Christian motivation. What Jesus asked for was the service which responds to need, which springs from caring and self-identification with the people who most need help.

2. *What price Charity?*

In the modern vocabulary, Charity has become an unfashionable word. It does not really deserve this treatment. Even in the Victorian era much charitable work sprang from genuine caring and concern. Within that context people like Shaftesbury, Wilberforce, Florence Nightingale and Josephine Butler were nurtured. In earlier centuries as in the missionary movement, Charity could be love in action and a very costly and demanding love too. It is however undeniable that it could also be a substitute for radical reform of social evils. Men gave 'of their superfluity' rather than of their own 'living'—as in the story of the poor widow and the rich donor in the Temple.

3. *The 'I and Thou' of service*

The real problem lies in the kind of relationship which charity or voluntary service conveys. It needs to be a relationship between people accepting each other as persons, with superiority or inferiority. Otherwise the recipient resents both the service and the one who gives it. One is reminded of two remarks: 'If you want to lose a friend, lend him money.' 'Why does he dislike me so much? I never did him a good turn!' There is uncomfortable truth here, as every social worker knows.

Treating each other as persons is something for which there is no substitute. From personal experience one can pay tribute to the outstanding generosity of the Dutch Reformed Churches in South Africa in their medical and welfare work for Africans. But the recipients of all this help ask for something more—for political freedom and for the recognition of basic human rights.

Even within the family, the issue can be evident. It can lie behind the question: 'I gave her everything—what more could she have wanted?' Perhaps 'things' were not enough to compensate for the withholding of love and value.

4. *The one who serves*

Look at this from the side of the giver. A generation ago Toc H familiarised us with the saying: 'Service is the rent we pay for our room on earth.' Nowadays in the welfare state we tend to reverse it to become: 'Service is the rent we expect from others for their room on earth.'

A person can go into marriage expecting the other partner to provide the service and the happiness, and both are disappointed. Our homes can be so child-centred, or so lacking in parental example of service to church or community, that youngsters come out into the world assuming it owes them everything. When it fails to behave as they expect it to do, they rebel or break down.

Yet on the other side of the picture it is evident that those who give service to others achieve a maturity of personality, one might even call it happiness although it is often at the cost of much self-denial, because they find meaning for their lives by helping others to find meaning in theirs.

5. Service in the Church

This situation asks us as Christians what quality of service we are willing to give each other within the Church and in the community. Our Lord washed feet. He 'came not to be ministered unto but to minister'. He gave service where others drew back in the most unrewarding situations among social rejects and misfits.

If Christianity is the imitation of Christ—and it dare not be less than that—then its service must be love in action, and in Ignatius Loyola's words, with no thought of any reward save that of knowing that we do God's will.

WHITSUNTIDE

The Church and harvest

Harvest Festivals as we know them today were invented just over a hundred years ago by an eccentric clergyman who had a passion for colour. He was married wearing a claret-coloured clerical coat, a blue jersey, hip-length wading boots and a pink hat. To his little parish of Morwenstow in Cornwall where he was Rector for 41 years from 1834, Robert Hawker brought gaiety and the colourful ceremonial of the Eastern Church of which he had scholarly knowledge. His revival of the harvest thanksgiving met a real need. It spread so rapidly throughout the country that in less than twenty years the Convocation of Canterbury found it necessary to issue special services.

What appealed to people was not just the colour and cheerfulness of the service or the singing of familiar hymns. Something deeper was involved, perhaps it was an expression of man's ancient sense of dependence on the processes of nature.

1. What does it mean now?

It may be questioned whether harvest will continue to mean anything to an increasingly urbanised civilisation confident that nothing can interrupt the flow of pre-packaged supplies.

But just as the war made people realise the vulnerability of their food supplies, so today we are beginning to see the harvest in a wider context in two important respects. One is associated with the word 'ecology' which has recently come into our popular vocabulary. We are learning that the balance of nature can be dangerously disturbed by the reckless use of pesticides and other techniques. We are realising that vast areas of productive land is being swallowed up for motorways, new towns, and new industrial areas.

The mass media are also compelling us to set out food requirements and our standards of living in a global context. Flood and famine, drought and soil erosion affect millions in Asia and Africa. A great proportion of the world's population live on the knife edge of subsistence. Men are questioning whether developments in scientific agriculture and food distribution can keep pace with the growth of world population.

In the international situation as in personal life, the words of John Donne ring true: 'No man is an island entire of himself.'

2. Come ye thankful people . . .

The modern harvest festival has therefore a new realism. And this was characteristic of the teaching of Jesus. He was never sentimental about the work on the land. His parables show his awareness of its demands and problems. He recognised the significance of interdependence and mutual co-operation in achieving the harvest. It embodied the principle of growth and the necessity of response to the providential activity of God. He saw thanksgiving, trust and sharing as basic to that response. If God cared so much even for the birds of the air and the beauty of the very weeds in the field, he asked, did He not care even more for human beings? Men must have faith in God and plan their lives accordingly, giving thanks for the essentials that made life possible.

3. *The harvest of life*

But Jesus was equally concerned about the harvest of a man's own life. The two aspects are related, for a man who cannot give thanks is usually one who gives others no cause to give thanks. Jesus gave the criterion by which people can be assessed more accurately than by their pretensions: 'By their fruits you shall know them.' By that standard what have any of us to show for our lives in terms of positive achievement and in the lives of other people? None of us can know the true answer to that question—yet. But one thing can give us a guide.

This is Christ's own principle of growth at the heart of the harvest. If we see the Christian life as a growth in spirit parallel with growth in mind and body, then we can expect 'productivity' in spiritual terms. The very idea of this may be disturbing. But there is nothing particularly holy about static religion of the kind which, for example, is content to pray 'the same prayers I said at my mother's knee', or responds to any call to new ventures of faith and service with complacent indifference.

Where the principle is accepted the results can be surprising. Of all the churches of the New Testament, the most outstanding was the one at Philippi. Generous in their contribution to the poverty-stricken church in Jerusalem, always loyal in their support of St Paul in prayer and money, and capable of making intellectual response to teaching of great theological depth, they were the Christians of whom the Apostle could write joyfully and gratefully: 'I thank God upon every remembrance of you.'

We pray that others may have reason to thank God upon every remembrance of us, the Church of Christ in this generation, growing in grace and in response to God.

THE WAY OF THE SPIRIT

The way of love

How can you tell a Christian? The answer, according to St Paul, lies in nine characteristics which are not just the results of human effort but of life lived 'in the Spirit'. In Galatians 5.22 & 23, he describes them as 'love, joy, peace, patience, gentleness, goodness, faith, meekness and self-control'. This is directly in line with the teachings of Jesus. But the question remains whether they are the characteristics that one should look for in the Christian today—or are they an impracticable ideal belonging to a by-gone age.

1. *The dangerous word*

The first 'fruit of the Spirit' is love. The word is used and abused to cover a wide variety of relationships, from the casual to the permanent, from the sentimental to sacrificial. We are dangerously familiar with it.

But Christ's use of the word was precise and demanding. In fact he gave four commandments about love—definite commands not mild exhortations.

2. *The first command*

Jesus endorsed the traditional command to love God 'with all thy heart, with all thy soul, with all thy mind and with all thy strength'. In other words, one is to love God with the whole of one's personality and being. To love Him with the mind means sharing with God one's worries as well as joys, ambitions as well as decisions. Love in the mind is a warm enthusiasm in sharing one's very thoughts with the Father.

To love God with one's strength is very demanding. One saint advised 'Do only that which thou canst offer to God'. This is not a kill-joy perfectionism but a creative principle if we apply it to the right use of abilities and opportunities. This is the Christian vocation which results in the joyful liberty of Christian obedience.

3. *The second command*

We might better understand the meaning of loving our neighbour as ourself if we reversed the clauses: 'Love yourself by all means but love your neighbour just as much.' Give your neighbour, as you give yourself, the same benefit of the doubt, the same concern about rights and happiness.

Who is my neighbour? In the original the word means literally 'The one next to you', whoever he may turn out to be. In the parable of the Good Samaritan, it is clear that the neighbour is not simply someone whom I ought to help, but the person whose help I myself may need. Loving my neighbour is not an act of condescension or enlightened self-interest. It belongs to my very humanity.

4. *The third command*

It was hard for the Jews to think of Samaritans in this relationship of neighbourliness. It must have been still harder for them to take Christ's injunction to love their enemies. The hatred of enemies—Romans, supporters of the 'permissive society' of Hellenism, publicans—was evidence of nationalist loyalty and religious orthodoxy. Christ's command is equally repugnant today to those who cling to group hatreds of class, colour, tribe, race or even religion. But love means seeing behind the label to the persons, as people or individuals like oneself.

That is just as important at the personal level where a man may claim that he has no enemies to love. But subconsciously I regard as my enemies those whom I fear, envy or distrust and those who compete with me for status or security or affection. They are the people to whom I attach a label as the Boss, the Shop Steward, The White Man, the Black, the Red, the Tory, the Delinquent or the Establishment. Because I think of someone as a Type, I cannot see him as a Person. But to Jesus, no one was a Type. No situation was a Case.

5. *The last command*

Because Jesus saw people in this way, he could give his disciples the supreme commandment about love, that they should love each other 'as I have loved you'. Whether men deserved it or not, responded or opposed, he loved others to the point of sacrifice even of life itself. He loved them as they were and did not give them the impression that he was trying to turn them into something different or manipulate them even for their own good. There was a supreme trust and liberty about the love of Jesus.

It is perfectly true that history has seen many instances of loving self-sacrifice among non-Christians as well as Christians. Christ's self-giving was for all humanity.

He asked it of his disciples as something of which he believed them to be capable, by the grace of God. That men should be capable of this kind of love is a ground of hope for humanity and, if one will accept it as such, it is a glimpse of the divine within the human soul.

The way of joy

THE AWKWARD QUESTION

If someone were to ask you 'Do you enjoy being a Christian?' would your answer be 'Yes?' If so, would this be supported by the impression you make on other people?

You might be the kind of person who would find it difficult to answer the question in the affirmative. Their religion makes some people acutely aware of their own faults, of the problems and sufferings of others and of the evil in the world. They might say that their religion gives them a certain inward peace and purpose, but hardly joy as such.

Yet if one looks closely at the Christianity of Jesus and his disciples, one has to recognise that it brought them a deep happiness despite their many problems.

1. The joy of Christ

On this very count Jesus was frequently criticised. He was condemned as the friend of wine-bibbers. He liked dining with his friends. He saw the funny side of life, too. One thinks of his gentle humour in dealing with Nathanael and with Zacchaeus. He enjoyed the beauties of nature. And when on that first Easter night he returned to his friends, the tremendous scene of St John 20 is marked by its joy.

That dozen young men all of his own age, thirty or so, would not have stayed with him for two demanding years unless they had enjoyed doing so. Then when the Church went into action at Pentecost it was not a community of fear but one of joy.

St Paul showed the same spirit. Looking back on his ministry, his acknowledged the many times of deep unhappiness, but the joy outweighed them all. He could thank God even for the suffering he had had to endure. From his own experience he could speak of joy as the gift of the Spirit.

2. The mark of the Church

Joy was one of the characteristics of Christianity which led to the rapid extension of the Church. The firmness of the religious faith of these early Christians, their courage in facing martyrdom and the attractiveness and purity of their family life, were all factors in this expansion. But even their enemies had to admit that there was a quality of happiness about them which aroused curiosity and won converts. It was evident even in their attitude to death. In the place of the sad farewells expressed in epitaphs on pagan tombs, there appeared the joyful assurance of reunion in inscriptions on Christian tombs in the catacombs.

It was not a superficial optimism blind to the harsh realities of life. The essence of Christian joy was its realism. They were well aware of their danger from outside. They faced up to the trials of moral lapse and heresy and conflict inside. But the Spirit could give them joy in believing and joy in life. This was because they possessed an inward security of faith and love in their relationship with the Risen Lord.

3. Does it work today?

Of course there are many ways in which we find joy in living, such as in our home and family, in our work, in things which give us aesthetic satisfaction and in our fellowship with others. They are usually activities which make some demand upon us and offer, in return, a kind of fulfilment. They also have about them a quality of permanence which distinguishes them from the things which simply give us pleasure. For the latter may satisfy temporary emotional demands, they may amuse or entertain, but we rarely expect more than that from them.

But one of the problems of our society is that although the circumstances of our life are so much more favourable than were those of past generations, yet there are so many people for whom life has no joy at all. The things which give them pleasure turn sterile. They are unable to make effective relationships with others. Loneliness or stress makes living unendurable and for some, suicide seems to be the only way out.

4. But what can Christianity offer?

This is a question Christians have to face. To ignore it is to live in a fools' paradise, blind to human need, as Bishop Gore put it when asked to say grace at a banquet during a time of economic depression: 'God forgive us for feasting while others are fasting.' The Christians must be involved in bringing some measure of the good life to others.

But he has to ask himself if he can do so if his own religion does not give him any joy to share. It is unfortunately true that frequently

Christianity gives the impression of dourness and cheerless fellow-ship, of nervous power-struggles within and little ability to deal with the stresses and strains of Christians in their private lives. Christians coming out of church can look as miserable as unsuccessful customers leaving a bingo hall!

The heart of the matter lies in one word *relationship*. Christian happiness is an enjoyable relationship with God and his world, with other people and even with oneself. It gives a sense of proportion which enables us to rejoice at the truth and beauty and goodness in the world, knowing that they are more real than the lies, the ugliness and the evil. It somehow helps us to see the best in people and to recognise in every situation that with God nothing is impossible. And with this sense of proportion goes a sense of humour which, not least in importance, prevents us taking ourselves too seriously.

THE WAY OF THE SPIRIT

The way of peace

'Shalom', the Hebrew word for peace, opened one of the most moving radio broadcasts of World War II. It came from a concentration camp where thousands of Jews had been put to death. The few survivors were in a state of ghastly emaciation. One heard their weak voices crying Shalom as they greeted the liberating troops. It was peace after agonies of suffering.

In the Old Testament peace meant more than a courteous greeting, or even freedom from war. It conveyed a sense of wholeness, of unity within oneself and with others and with God. It was seen as a gift from God and would be the outstanding characteristic of the Messianic Kingdom where swords would be beaten into ploughshares and spears into pruning hooks. The disorder of nature would be done away. The enmity among men would disappear.

The same emphasis on the positive nature of peace appears in the New Testament where Christ is its agent and the Spirit is its power. Peace is never depicted as a kind of escape from life. It happens in the midst of life as it has to be lived now. It is the fruit of reconciliation.

1. Did Jesus practise what he preached?

Jesus said: 'Blessed are the peacemakers, for they shall be called the children of God'. But there were many who saw him as far from being a peacemaker. The Jewish and Roman authorities regarded him as a dangerous trouble-maker. Others may have criticised him as a disturber of family life. They heard him actually say that he came not to bring peace but a sword, to set members of families against each other for the sake of the Gospel.

The New Testament itself foreshadows the disruptive effects of his Gospel and the pages of history are scarred by religious wars. Conflict over religion has broken families and communities and shattered individual personality. We can see the 'sword', but where is the peace?

2. The peace of the Gospel

Jesus said 'My peace I give unto you, not as the world gives. 'Let not your heart be troubled, neither let it be afraid.' He knew that the enemies of peace within the individual are insecurity, fear and lack of trust. His words about worry are significant. He said 'Be not anxious about the morrow'. The word 'anxious' is literally 'split-minded', the confusion of mind which makes it difficult for us to use the present to the full. The confident acceptance of the daily situation was evident in Jesus himself and his disciples learned its secret from him. As St John puts it in his first Epistle: 'Perfect love casts out fear because fear has torment.' The love of God was the root of confidence which gave unity and wholeness.

When the Christian had achieved peace in his inner life he could move out to bring peace to the outside world. But first he must live in unity with his fellow-members in Christ. For the Church to be an agent of reconciliation, it must itself be reconciled. This is emphasized in every one of St Paul's letters and he had no illusions about the difficulty of putting this into practice. The standard was clear: 'There is neither Jew nor Greek, bond or free, male or female, for you are all one in Christ Jesus.'

But it could not be a superficial unity. The Jewish-Gentle controversy soon dominated the life of the early Church. St Peter was prepared to compromise for the sake of a kind of peace. St Paul had to challenge him, believing as he did that unity must be complete. He acted in the same way in the churches of his own foundation when principle—which was often a label for prejudice

—or divisions of class or custom, demanded a constant awareness of the vocation of the Church. It could not offer a way of reconciliation and of peace to a broken world if it was itself disunited. This same challenge presents itself to us today.

3. The gift and the receiver

In the life of the Church peace is the gift of the Spirit but implementing it demands sacrifice. It is the same in the life of the individual. If I really want to experience 'the peace that passes human understanding' then I must allow the Spirit to remove from my life the elements which make war—the pride and prejudice, the groundless fears and worries, the habits of mind which are even more important than habits of body. It is not sufficient for me to want peace in most of my life while clinging to the elements of conflict in some particular department of my being. For peace needs wholeness of response if it is to last, and if it is to give one that spiritual security which can resist the disruptive pressures from outside. Here Colossians 3.15 gives sound advice: 'Let the peace of God act as judge in your hearts.' For it is in the many decisions of daily life that we actually make, or break, peace.

No one can deny that peace is the desperate need of the world today, not only between nations and groups, but also in personal life. Half the hospital beds of our country are occupied by people in mental stress. Thousands of families are broken by conflicts, many of which need never have happened. Whatever service the Church and the Christian can give, it must surely include the ministry of peace conveying the help of the Spirit.

THE WAY OF THE SPIRIT

The way of patience

The gods of the Greeks were an impatient company. They were quick to take offence, somewhat lavish with thunderbolts, always ready to punish the 'hubris', the presumption of mortal cleverness which threatened their own supremacy. So deity was usually as quick-tempered as it was unpredictable.

The God of Israel, on the other hand, was usually presented by the prophets as a deity of infinite patience, although in the Old

Testament there are traces of earlier ideas of God's quick resentment of sacrilege and breaches of taboo.

But the prophets portrayed God as so loving Israel that he endured the unreliability of his people. He made the Covenant and kept it although Israel broke it frequently. As a husband with his unfaithful wife, God's long-suffering was proof of his love, just as it is in human relations in any age. Our ability to put up with the major faults or the minor irritants in others depends on whether we really love them. To extend this to people outside the circle of family or friends demands two things. One is the willingness to see ourselves in a caring relationship with them. The other, according to St Paul, is the particular gift of the Spirit which develops in us that patience which, in the New Testament meaning of it, is 'the long holding-out of the mind before it gives room to passion.'

1. *The impatient world*

We live, as Christ did, in an impatient world. To strike first and ask questions later, becomes the rule in many conflicts between nations and groups. Within family life, there is similar precipitate action and rapid breakdown occurs even though the point of disagreement may seem trivial. The tensions of modern life are blamed for what has been called the 'battered baby syndrome' and much other cruelty within the home. Impatience is believed to be a major factor in road accidents also.

There is another side to this problem of patience, in its Authorised Version translation as 'long-suffering'. For ours is a generation which cannot accept suffering and takes refuge to an extent greater than ever before in tranquillizers and other drugs. We want instant relief just as we demand instant success. Long, patient and self-sacrificing endeavour is as unfamiliar as is the acceptance of suffering.

2. *The patience of Jesus*

The Christian understanding of this element in the Way must begin with the example of Jesus. At first sight he appears to have been violent and radical in his demands for reform as he cleansed the Temple and condemned the hypocrisy of the Scribes and Pharisees. But it is the mark of patience which is most characteristic of his ministry.

For years after reaching manhood he waited until the right time for his mission had arrived. Patiently he trained his disciples for Apostleship, enduring their slowness of understanding and their repeated failures. We cannot begin to understand what he bore so patiently during that week of the Passion, betrayed by his friends, victim of an unjust trial and murdered by those he tried to help.

He called his disciples to the same endurance, offering a cross instead of earthly success, and warning that the way would be long and hard. He asked them to wait and watch for things to happen in God's good time. They had to be patient with God as well as patient with men.

3. Is it still valid?

Patience with God and with people is one thing. But impatience with evil is the other-side of the Christian mission. The Gospel challenges us to be impatient about the real evils in human society which corrupt the minds of men and manipulate them as though they were things. And impatience means action, not merely protest. This is the consequence which the Church must face if it really is concerned about the redemption of human society and human nature. Resolution is more important than resolutions.

The same applies in personal life. Patience with people is one of the most significant contributions which the individual Christian may be called upon to make in the tensions and strains of modern living. Perhaps one help in achieving this is the remembrance of how much patience has been shown towards oneself by other people—one's parents, teachers, husband or wife . . . yes, even by one's children. (There is a flash of inspired advice in Colossians 3.21 telling fathers not to exasperate their children!)

4. The divine patience

But there has been the patience of God with you and me throughout the years. There have been times when we were in a hurry, and God was not. At other times we have behaved as Israel did all those centuries ago, and God went on caring and forgiving and waiting. So when I am tempted to be impatient with others and with life itself, I am brought back to sanity by the memory of God's long-suffering to me throughout my life. If I am to be justifiably impatient it must be with the sin within myself and this demands action, not mere regret.

So patience is to be seen not as just a virtue, an ideal beyond achievement. It is God's sharing with us an attitude to life and to

84

people which is part of the divine being. It is a gift of Himself in this gift of the Spirit.

THE WAY OF THE SPIRIT

The way of kindness

Of all the descriptions of Christ in the New Testament, one with a particular charm is St Paul's phrase in his letter to Titus: 'The kindness of God'. There was nothing sentimental about this. St Paul was describing the Incarnation as God in his infinite power and compassion coming down to meet the deepest needs of humanity. He was asking that in their dealings with one another men should reflect the nature of God and exercise that kindness which was His gift to them.

1. *How kind was Jesus?*

Most of us think of our Lord in terms of the children's hymns as 'Gentle Jesus, meek and mild'. But there were times when he was quite different from this. Faced with the indifference of the Scribes and the Pharisees to the problems of ordinary people, his criticisms of them were blunt and devastating. He said that those who corrupted children were better dead. Even his friends could be treated sharply. At Caesarea Philippi Peter tried to dissuade him from the way of suffering. Jesus said abruptly: 'Get behind me, Satan.'

Jesus knew that there are times in life when kindness in the ordinary sense of the word, can be mistaken. He was not afraid to 'speak the truth in love' even if it hurt.

Frequently people develop a wrong pattern of life just because at a formative period in their lives no one had the kindness to be unkind and honest to them. A young man in his first job drifted into dishonesty. He was saved from disaster by his family making sacrifices to repay the money he had stolen. The same thing happened again and again. Eventually he came to complete ruin when the family were no longer at hand to rescue him. They had been too kind.

Looking back on life one recognises how much one owes to people who care enough to bring one up sharply with a stiff word of criticism or correction. It may have seemed unkind at the time but it was necessary. It is not enough just to 'learn from experience'. Sometimes someone has to show us what to learn—someone who cares enough to take the trouble to do so.

This caring and understanding was typical of Jesus. He was sensitive to the unexpressed longing of Nathaniel which lay behind the rather glib question 'Can any good thing come out of Nazareth?' He understood the 'hot and bothered' exasperation of Martha with her sister. Even when he knew that Judas was going to betray him, Jesus did not expose him to the wrath of his disciples. He showed no resentment of the soldiers who were nailing him to the cross.

This was 'the kindness of God' in action. It was a virtue, not of weakness but of strength.

2. Caring about people

What was outstanding about the kindness of Jesus was its universality. It was not confined, as ours might be, to his immediate friends and people from whom he could expect a similar return. It flowed out to people in any situation, from what was essential—a continuing and warm attitude to others. He cared about them as individuals.

This is of particular importance today because of the impersonality of life. It would be untrue to say that people are more unkind than were their forefathers. One has only to think of the ghoulishness of public executions, legal systems protecting property rather than people so that children could be transported for a trivial theft, the exploitation of child-labour, and the savagery of wars including those in the name of religion. The kindness of our ancestors was as qualified as is our own.

Ours is a difference of situation rather than of degree. It is harder for people to show the kindness they need because they do not know each other. The young couple starting family life in the concrete jungle of a great city, the old person isolated from relatives and friends, the families uprooted from familiar neighbourhoods to be replanted in vast conurbations, the woman trying to bring up her child by herself, the hospital patient who has no family to visit him . . . the welfare state may provide for their physical needs. But they want something more—to know that they matter to someone who is personally interested in them. Many of the suicides of our time are attributed to loneliness in a society which seems to de-personalize human beings.

3. *The personal response*

Where do we begin? Jesus told us to begin with our neighbour, the person next to one, the immediate and even the casual contact. And it works that way. The nurse who cheerfully endures the petulance of any of us as hospital patients secretly more disturbed than we would admit, the family that puts up with grandfather's cantankerousness, the grandfather trying to bridge the generation gap, the policeman patiently dealing with the nervous immigrant... there are so many who make an immense difference to the lives of others by their kindness.

What they are revealing is that true kindness is not an act of condescension. It is a recognition of kinship. The two words Kind and Kin are from the same root. They are related in life as well as in the dictionary. As Jesus taught, we belong to each other and kindness is the practical realisation of our fundamental belonging in common humanity under God.

THE WAY OF THE SPIRIT

The way of goodness

THE VICTORIAN IDEAL

Charles Kingsley wrote:
'Be good, sweet maid, and let who can be clever.'
This kind of advice was popular a century ago in the time of Queen Victoria who, as a young girl promised 'I will be good'. There is no record of anyone having asked her to define what she meant by the adjective. She might simply have been reflecting the contemporary idea of the model child as one 'seen but not heard', obedient and pious, and certainly free from that wilful individualism, the eradication of which was the prime object of education.

The man she married came to be known as Albert the Good. Here the appellation was somewhat more positive. Albert won it by his deep sympathy with the conditions of the working classes and by his sound advice which helped to avert war with the United States in 1861. But our general impression of that era is of one which had clear but limited ideas of good and evil and was convinced that it knew the difference between them.

1. Goodness in question

The Victorian age stands in sharp contrast with our own. We are confused about right and wrong but disinclined to accept the experience and the value-judgements of the past. Indeed, we are reluctant to accept any general standards at all. We assume that every man is the best judge of morals and is capable of deciding for himself in any situation.

We go further. We suspect those who try to live a good life or to do good to others, of doing so for wrong reasons. They may be trying to cover up their deeper urges or to achieve compensation for their inadequacy, through power and status. So on the surface, goodness as such is out of fashion.

But there is another side to this. People long to find integrity in their leaders and fidelity in their relationships. Even in a climate of selfishness, men and women are capable of honesty and self-sacrifice. Beneath the surface of pleasure fixation and materialism, they look for the good life in meaningful relationships. They feel that happiness depends on what one is and not on what one has. And in all this they are very close to the goodness which St Paul believed men could achieve by the help of the Spirit, which was the goodness they had seen in the life of Christ.

2. The goodness of Jesus

To Jesus, goodness was a theological virtue. That is to say, it proceeded from the nature of God. In St Mark 10.18, we have an example of his precision in using the word. A young man asked him the question: 'Good Master, what shall I do that I may inherit eternal life?' Jesus replied: 'Why do you call me good? There is no one good except God'. He went on to challenge the young man about his keeping of the commandments. He assured Jesus that he had kept them ever since youth. Then Jesus, looking compassionately at him, said that he needed only one thing and that was to give away all his wealth to the poor and then follow Christ, taking up his cross. To give up this barrier to complete goodness and to the life of the kingdom, was too much for the man and he went sadly away.

Then Jesus told his disciples that it would be hard for the wealthy to enter the Kingdom. This amazed them. They had been brought up to regard wealth as a proof of divine approval, not as an impediment to the spiritual life. Jesus' statement upset their ideas of goodness and providence.

But he upset their ideas about goodness in other respects. They had thought of it in terms of ritual cleanness and religious obligations such as prayer and fasting. He depicted it in terms of service and compassion flowing out of the heart of a man, the very place where evil also originated. St Mark 7.22 & 23 is very blunt about this, saying that from within the human personality 'proceed evil thoughts, adulteries, fornications, murders, thefts, covetousness, wickedness, deceit, lasciviousness, an evil eye, blasphemy, pride and foolishness.'

Our Lord singled out one sign as beyond forgiveness. This was the sin against the Holy Spirit—the deliberate choice of evil and rejection of goodness.

This element of choice is fundamental to goodness as Jesus saw it. It was not the negative abstention from evil. It was the whole personality, desiring the good and achieving it by the help of the Holy Spirit.

3. *The will to goodness*

Archbishop Temple wrote: 'I can be good if I want to. The trouble is that I don't always want to.' St Paul lamented that the evil which he did not want to do, he kept on doing. But the good he wanted to do, he could not do. He described this condition as a slavery of the soul from which only Christ could deliver him.

This is reflected in our own lives. It is not enough to experience what has been called 'the divine dissatisfaction with oneself', or to yearn to be free of our besetting sins. Something is necessary to unite the mind and the emotions and the will so as to choose the good and achieve it.

This is what St Paul called the power of the Spirit and the 'being in Christ'. For Christ himself supplies not only the true standard by which we can distinguish between good and evil but also the strength by which to make the choice and live by it.

THE WAY OF THE SPIRIT

The way of faith

1. *The crisis of faith*

What is wrong with modern man? The answer some people give to this question is that man is going through a crisis of faith, that, in fact, he has lost faith in himself, in his neighbour and in God.

Even within the churches this crisis is apparent. The Bible is under fire. Traditional forms of authority are no longer accepted without question. Fundamental doctrines are no longer sacrosanct or are tacitly ignored. The Apostles' Creed, for instance, contains about twenty statements of belief. One might ask how many of these are said with conviction and commitment by a congregation or by the individual Christian, during a church service in which the saying of the Creed is the central affirmation of the faith.

Some might ask if this matters. It might reasonably be argued that the important point is that we should have a basic faith in God which does not need detailed definition. Another argument is that more significant than Christian doctrine is the Christian conduct which shows itself in good neighbourliness, sound moral standards and the readiness to be of service to others. These are valuable but the difficulty is that this kind of 'practical Christianity' may be of little avail in times of crisis or temptation. Moreover, what really determines our conduct is the belief and the set of values which lies beneath the surface of our activities and relationships. It is not so much what we do that is of paramount importance, as the underlying motive for our doing it. If our faith is weak then our behaviour can go astray and our good works become superficial.

This is what the writers of the New Testament were deeply concerned about. When St Paul wrote to the Galatians, he was opposing the view that salvation came from doing the works of the Law. Centuries later, the Reformers challenged the belief that salvation came from doing the works of the inner life of the Church. Today we are in danger of thinking that salvation comes from doing the works of the Church in society. Many are uneasy about our 'activism' and believe that we are being recalled to recognise the priority of faith in the life of the Church.

2. What do we believe about man?

When attempting to define the faith, we usually start by thinking about God. But in his mission to the world, Jesus often began with man, demonstrating in his teaching and his actions what he believed about human nature and its needs. He valued people as individuals in need of each other and in need of God. He treated them as human beings who were responsible and able to respond to very real demands upon their time, their efforts and their love. He was acutely aware of human frailty and did not hesitate to locate the root of man's troubles and sins within his own personality, not in his outward contacts or his environment. Jesus attributed to man the highest value ever given him, when he described him as the child of God, and called him to fulfil his sonship in the Kingdom.

This is the basis of the Christian faith in man. But some aspects of it have to be set in the context of what man has come to know about himself in recent years. The main problem is in respect of human freedom. Scientific studies tend to be deterministic and to hold that man is conditioned to an extent greater than he realises by factors in his mind and body and his social environment, of which he is not aware. The Christian faith holds that whatever may be the factors and pressures bearing upon him, ultimately man makes the decisions and should be regarded as a responsible person —who needs the help of God in making those decisions. One appreciates that this is an over-simplification of the issue but nevertheless it is on this point that the argument turns.

Furthermore, what men believe about their own nature affects their belief about their neighbours. My faith in others is a projection of my faith in myself. That is sometimes painfully apparent when I am critical of my neighbour. And when I ask 'What is Man?', I am really asking 'Who am I?' My answer to that question reflects at the same time what I believe about God.

3. *What do we believe about God?*

Central in the Christian faith is the belief that in Jesus Christ we have the true revelation both of human nature and of the nature of God. If one asks what God is like, one turns for answer to the teaching of Jesus, but also to the character of Jesus. And here one finds no evasion of the questions about God which man asks in every age out of the heart of human tragedy, about the purpose of life, the meaning of innocent suffering, the price of human freedom and the apparent silence of God in the face of the victory of evil. This is not a Gospel of 'God's in his heaven—All's right with the world!' or of the distant Old Man Up There. This is the God who cares enough to be among men, who trusts them enough to give them freedom, who acts only when they want him to do so with their whole will.

This is where the Christian faith in God begins. But it does not end there. Jesus led his disciples to make new discoveries about God. He promised them that the Holy Spirit would continue to lead them in the venture of faith. That promise holds good today. We must not be afraid to open our minds to new revelations about

91

God and His world. The exploration of space and the investigation of human life do not threaten the existence of God. But they challenge us to ask if our idea of God is too small. Our faith must be as unlimited as God's universe.

THE WAY OF THE SPIRIT

The way of meekness

THE OUT-OF-DATE VIRTUE

Who would want to hear a sermon on 'Meekness'? The very word conjures up the memory of Charles Dickens' oily villain, Uriah Heep; or else it brings back another Victorian memory of stained glass windows depicting the meek-and-mild Jesus with unattractive sentimentality.

Nowadays we replace it with the virtue of self-confidence. We should be very unlikely to employ an applicant for a job whose testimonial described him as meek.

1. *The meekness of Jesus*

The curious thing is that meekness figured so prominently in the New Testament. Jesus included it in the Beatitudes saying 'Blessed are the meek; for they shall inherit the earth'. He deliberately emphasized it as the keynote of his messiahship in the mode of his Palm Sunday entry. As a child being presented in the Temple, he was revealed first of all to Simeon and Anna. They were typical of the humble and godly folk who were awaiting 'the consolation of Israel.' Mary's Magnificat went back to the Incarnation and recalled the meekness which was characteristic of God's self-revelation.

When writing, to the Philippians, St Paul described meekness and humility not as optional extras but as essential to the mode of the Incarnation of Christ who had emptied himself of his glory and became 'obedient unto death'. And he spoke of meekness not as a matter of outward demeanour but as a way of life for the whole personality, which could be achieved by the power of the Spirit.

One might be tempted to dismiss this as merely a counsel of perfection. But Jesus had no illusions about meekness. He knew how hard it was to achieve this in any community including that of his disciples. He knew how vulnerable it made a man to the aggression and competitiveness of his own or any other age. But he was somehow convinced of the ultimate victory of the meek. Was he being realistic?

2. *Can meekness win?*

At first sight meekness seems hopelessly out of place in our own time which is as violent and aggressive as was the first century. We have political liberation movements, civil rights agitation, industrial action, guerrilla groups, power blocks and mass movements and they have no place for the meek. These are the ones who suffer when there are strikes. They become the homeless casualties of war and tribal conflict. They are the air-liner passengers hijacked by the world's ideologies. If they try to withstand the group, they are accused of being anti-social and traitors to the cause. If they want to be accepted then they must go with the tide, sacrificing their integrity and their principles.

But meekness is not the same as surrender or apathy. This is the mistake which has often been made throughout Christian history. Sometimes the Church has bought security by turning a blind eye to dangerous developments in the State. Sometimes it has abstained from involvement assuming a 'holier-than-thou' attitude.

Yet there is a theological and positive side to meekness. It starts from obedience to what is sincerely believed to be the will and purpose of God. This obligation may well lead Christians to say 'No!' to the demands of Caesar, and to be prepared to pay the price for doing so. The power of meekness is well understood by the omnicompetent State even if Christians do not see it equally clearly. What the atheistic or totalitarian State fears is not the physical power of the Church but the spiritual and moral power of its obedience to God. In the long run, it is the battle for men's minds that matters most. And meekness implicitly and explicitly asks fundamental questions about means as well as ends, about truth and about the nature of man himself. These very questions ultimately undermine the authority of the power which seeks to silence them.

3. *Meekness and the self*

But one might ask if the blessedness of the meek is apparent in personal life. Does it really 'inherit the earth?' Jesus asked: 'What

93

shall it profit a man if he shall gain the whole world, and lose his own soul?'

We may not seek to gain the whole world. But if we examine what we want most from life we may find our ambitions taking the form of success and power, status or possessions. At a deeper level we may look for fulfilment in our work, and in our relationships. Now we are getting near to the truth. For the most important world is one of relationships, of loving and being loved. It is here that meekness matters in the form of a basic humility which is not negative and self-destructive but positive and productive. In love there cannot be room for self-assertion and aggressiveness. When we work with others in friendship and fellowship, we can do so effectively only if our concern for others, and for the cause we jointly serve, outweighs merely selfish considerations.

Then we know the blessedness of which Christ spoke. And we have seen it in people. Those who achieve most seem to have a quietly confident sense of purpose. They are not anxious about status or the recompense of appreciation. Because they are inwardly secure, they are not touchy and over-sensitive, or reluctant to give credit to others. The service they render matters more than its rewards for themselves. They do not suffer from the 'analysis-paralysis' of our time which constantly looks in the mirror of life to ask 'Who am I? What am I getting out of life? What are my rights?'

Yet there is nothing negative about their lives. They are, in fact, enthusiasts for goodness and sometimes they take an unexpectedly firm stand on what they believe to be a matter of principle. Moreover, they seem to enjoy life despite the problems which they have to face. They would be astonished to find themselves described as Saints. Yet that is exactly what they are. They are the real power of the Church, the meek who are the ultimate barrier to evil when it seeks to inherit the earth. For they live by that love of which, in 1 Corinthians 13, 5–7, St Paul wrote: 'It is not puffed up, does not behave itself unseemly, seeks not its own, is not easily provoked, thinks no evil; rejoices not in iniquity, but rejoices in the truth; bears all things, hopes all things and endures all things.' Love is the power of the meekness which is victorious.

The way of self-control

Seven centuries before Christ when the pagan world wanted guidance, it consulted the Oracle at Delphi in Greece. Frequently the advice given incorporated one or other of two sayings: 'Know Thyself.' 'No Excess'. Such counsel was not always what people had expected to receive or what they would welcome. Much the same thing may have happened when, as in Galatians 5.23, St Paul wrote of self-control as the last of the fruits of the Spirit.

Jewish Christians already knew this to be one of their religious obligations. They had been brought up to regard fasting and alms-giving as required by the Mosaic Law. The Jews were very critical of the self-indulgence of the heathen world. They were disgusted by the promiscuity and prostitution practised at pagan temples—as indeed it had also been evident at the 'high places' of Palestine. They were shocked by the orgies at the royal palaces. They resented the cult of the body which Hellenism was bringing into their own country.

Gentile Christians, however, could have grown up in a different atmosphere. It would have been hard for them to realise that it was utterly opposed to true Christianity. Many of them held on to the old ways even after becoming Christians. The first Epistle to Timothy ranges over many aspects of intemperance—drunkenness, violent quarrelling, lying, abusive language, self-conceit and greed.

St Paul never hesitated to challenge this low standard of personal life. But he also set a standard for himself which demonstrated the ideal which he preached. Writing to the Corinthians, he took his analogy from the Games which meant as much to them as do national sports in countries today. He asked that men should train for religion as they trained for athletics. He included mastery of the body adding the warning which clergy and ministers have always found acutely pertinent to their own situation: 'I keep under my body and bring it into subjection, last that by any means when I have preached to others, I myself should be a castaway.'

1. *Temperance goes astray*

It was perhaps inevitable that men should take this teaching to one extreme or the other. Even in New Testament times some held that Christianity demanded abstention from marriage and from certain kinds of food and drink because they were evil in themselves.

This arose from a form of dualism which held that the body, which was corrupt, was the prison of the soul, which was essentially pure. The purpose of self-control was essentially selfish.

Some went to the other extreme. They argued that self-indulgence even to excess could do them no harm because their souls were saved and therefore safe. Others have tended to think that religion is basically concerned with things spiritual and mental and that bodily abstinence is of little importance.

In short, through the centuries there has been a tension of principles and practices. On the one hand it has been argued that abstinence is necessary for the sake of spiritual development and of witness to the world. On the other hand, it has been maintained that it is right to make full use of all that God has given us in the world of His creation.

2. What is the right way?

Nowadays the argument runs along different lines. The Church is criticised for having given the impression of being hostile to the enjoyment of the good things of life and obsessed with questions of sex. It is argued that self-restraint is psychologically harmful. Freedom to express oneself is more important than self-control. One need not elaborate on the consequences of this attitude which can be as harmful to the individual as they are to those who live with him.

But the Gospel thinks differently. It has never been a religion of hatred of the self. It believes that God is the creator of everything including the body and its instincts. They are in themselves morally neutral, capable of being used for good or for evil. But it teaches that what matters most is the purpose for which the self exists. This is what should determine our use of God's created gifts, in what we eat and drink, in our attitude to sex and to all other relationships.

Moreover although the Gospel said little about these aspects of the matter which seem of such concern to modern man, it said a lot about the self-control which counts most—that is the self-control of the mind. The philosopher Descartes wrote 'Cogito ergo sum'—I think, therefore I am. One could take this a step further and say 'What I think, I am'.

The control of the body must begin with thinking straight, as the Delphic Oracle advised, with true self-knowledge. But this is not quite enough.

Tennyson wrote:
  'Self-reverence, self-knowledge, self-control,
  These three alone lead life to sovereign power.'
That is only part of the truth. And we know it. The real power that matters, which is the power over oneself, can only come with the help of God, which St Paul called the gift of the Spirit.

PERSONAL EXPERIENCE

Where is your treasure? (Moses)

1. A study in management

Management Studies are a feature of the modern business world. But the first 'case-history' on management is to be found in the Old Testament, in Exodus 18.

This was the situation. Moses had brought the Israelites out of Egypt and into the Wilderness. Then his father-in-law, Jethro, arrived bringing with him Moses' wife Zipporah and their two sons. So there was a happy family reunion. The next day Jethro went out to see the vast camp. He found Moses sitting in judgement. From morning to evening long queues of people waited to consult him on a variety of matters, from a decision between a man and his neighbour, to a detailed exposition of religious law.

Jethro commented bluntly: 'What you are doing is not good. You will surely wear away yourself and the people too.' He advised Moses to stick to his proper job, to be mediator for the people to God as well as leader. He should organise a system using carefully selected able and godly men, to be 'rulers of thousands, hundreds, fifties and tens.' They would handle day-to-day affairs and bring to Moses only what Jethro described as 'great matters'.

In modern terms, Jethro was advising his son-in-law to establish his priorities and to delegate responsibility in the light of them. Moses had the wisdom, and the greatness, to accept the advice. He did not object that the proposal threatened his status. He did not feel that he was indispensable at all levels of control. He did not cling to his problem while complaining about it—as is so often the case with those who seem to have a love-hate relationship with their burdens of responsibility. And, incidentally, one reason why he took his father-in-law's advice was that between the two men there was a common basis of mutual trust and of faith in God. So the one could ask the right questions and the other could face them.

2. *The question of priorities*

This event took place over three thousand years ago. But Jethro's counsel is relevant today, particularly to those in positions of leadership in the Church or in the community at large. It is dangerously easy for anyone with such responsibilities, whether bishop, clergyman or layman, to be too busy to examine what should be his priorities. The 'Martha Complex' is easily acquired by any of us.

Moses was challenged to give first place to the Godward aspect of his ministry, and so are we. From that vocation all other ministry is derived. The first call upon any church is to be the instrument of God. We can test how far that is being fulfilled in our local situation by examining the agenda of our church meetings. Most of them start with prayer, but is the Holy Spirit really free to operate only under Any Other Business when the rest of the agenda is cut and dried already?

It is always essential for the Church to have the right priorities but it is vitally important for it to do so today when the world at large is confused about them. Millions are uneasy about this matter. Two world wars in one generation have shaken their faith in man's ability to make peace and keep it. They marvel at the scientific outreach into space but measure the vast expense of this against the needs of the starving millions of people. They submit to the mass-society but resent its dehumanizing effects upon themselves. They suspect that the highest priority is being given to planning and profitability at the expense of people as persons in their own right.

3. *First things first*

There is the same confusion in personal life, where false values produce stress and breakdown, freedom degenerates into licence and the cult of individualism breaks up family life. When men are obsessed with status and possessions, with power and profit, their achievement can destroy themselves and others in the long run. This is exactly what Jesus forecast in the passage in the Sermon on the Mount (St Matthew 6.19–21) on the treasures on which man sets store. He was stating a plain fact when he said: Where your treasure is, there will your heart be also'. The ultimate determinant

of a man's life is his treasure, that which consciously or unconsciously is most important to him. The problem is that he is often
unaware of its true nature. A father, for example, may be too busy
making money for his children's future to spare them any time in
the present. A husband or wife may be generous with tokens of
affection, but mean with love itself.

4. *Where is the treasure?*

Jesus linked the treasure with the heart and this is significant. The
strongest power in the world is love. A man identifies himself
with what he loves. The object can be self-centred in terms of
money, power or status. It can be other-centred in terms of his
family or humanity or some cause to which he devotes himself.
This will be the treasure that like a lode-stone affects the compass of
his decisions and choices.

What Jesus was setting out in his Gospel and in his life was the
treasure of true happiness and fulfilment which man could achieve
by the response of love to God and neighbour. It was not an attitude
of superficial benevolence but a love which could be costly and
demand the sacrifice of which human nature at its best is capable by
the grace of God.

This is at the heart of the Gospel and in the long run it is the
ultimate criterion by which all other priorities must be assessed.
For it says simply that People matter more than Things and God
matters most of all. And in man's heart he know this to be true.

PERSONAL EXPERIENCE

The problem of power (David)

We move nowadays from one power crisis to another. Coal, oil,
petrol, electricity and atomic fuel are essential to the running of an
increasingly sophisticated and mechanised civilisation. We are
told that we are using up reserves faster than they can be replaced.
At the same time the supplies of power are so vulnerable to political
or industrial action that the economic life of a nation can be arrested
by the action of a determined minority.

But even more important than the crisis in material power is the
crisis in power over people. We have seen the rise of totalitarian
states claiming absolute authority over people's lives, eliminating

opposition, destroying freedom and manipulating truth. Yet even within the so-called free society massive power-structures have developed and the freedom of the individual is severely limited. The only possibility of participation lies in the ballot-box. But even that can be reduced to a formality by ignorance and apathy on the one hand and by the pressure of propaganda on the other. The planned society demands more and more power over people. What it dislikes, however, is being asked the question: 'Power to what end?' It usually answers it in terms of growth, efficiency or progress. What it is reluctant to do is to evaluate its power in terms of people and accountability.

1. *What is power for?*

The double problem of the purpose and the accountability of power is cogently illustrated in the Old Testament in two incidents in the life of David.

The first occurs in 2 Samuel 23. With a handful of supporters David was hiding in the cave of Adullam from the Philistines who were in possession of Bethlehem. He expressed a longing for a drink of water from the well in his home village. Three of his friends fought their way through the enemy lines to get the water for him. When they came back with it, David did not drink it. Instead he poured it upon the ground as a thank-offering to God for the service and self-sacrifice of his friends. They would not have interpreted this as a quixotic gesture. They saw it as evidence of his reluctance to satisfy his need at the possible cost of the lives of his friends. This refusal to abuse his power over others was typical of David at his best.

But there was another side to his character shewn when after he became King, he seduced Bathsheba, the wife of Uriah the Hittite, one of his army commanders. She became pregnant. When David failed to cover up his guilt, he ordered that Uriah should be abandoned in the front of the battle to be slain by the enemy. The device succeeded. David took Bathsheba into his household. Their son was born. That seemed the end of the matter. It would hardly have aroused comment in the case of the absolute monarchs of other countries at that time. The King could do no wrong. His power was absolute.

Then the prophet Nathan appeared. He told of a rich man who seized and killed a poor man's lamb to provide a meal for a visitor. David was furious and pronounced severe judgement against the rich man 'because he had no pity'. And Nathan said: 'You are the man.' He went on to pronounce God's judgement against the king.

David accepted the judgement with penitence. His kingship was of a kind unique in the ancient world. He was king by his own achievement and by popular choice. But even more he was king by covenant, the anointed of God and answerable to God. And he knew it.

2. *The challenge of power*

These two incidents show the most important aspects of the right use of power as Christ himself saw them—its respect for persons and its accountability to God. These are the two guiding principles which must apply as much in the affairs of the community and of the nations, as in our relationships as individual. Every 'power structure' including that of the Church must be assessed by these two standards and be challenged if it fails to observe them. That challenge may have to involve political and social action and we cannot ignore this possibility by taking refuge in the mis-application of the text 'The powers that be are ordained of God'. All too often evil forces have gained control of nations not least because the Church refused to act effectively when they were in their early stages of development.

It is equally important that we should not ignore the implications of the power we wield in personal life. Practically every one of us has some influence on the lives of others. This is obviously so in the case of parents or teachers, leaders in the political or commercial or academic life of a country, or people who mould public opinion through the mass-media. The use of their power depends on their value of people, and their control of self-interest. And behind these lies their concern for truth—including the truth, as Christians would see it, of their accountability to God. For this was both the promise and the warning which Jesus gave in his picture of Judgement. Then, he said, we shall all be judged by what we have done in our lives with the power to help or harm or to ignore the needs of our fellow-men. We shall know then that power is not a possession but a stewardship from God.

PERSONAL EXPERIENCE

Solomon's choice

The reign of Solomon began with a situation like that of a fairy tale. In a dream, the young king heard God offering him anything he wanted—long life, riches or power over his enemies. Solomon asked for none of these things. Instead he told God that he was aware of his youth, his inexperience and his great responsibilities. He realised that what he needed most was 'an understanding heart, to judge the people, and distinguish between good and bad.' In his dream he heard God praise him for his choice and promise to give him also the power and glory and long life for which he had not asked. But there was one condition—that Solomon should walk in God's ways, to keep His statutes and commandments.

1. *The first test*

In 1 Kings 3.16, it is recorded that Solomon's power of discernment was tested almost immediately. Two harlots came before him. The child of one of them had died but both claimed a surviving child to be her own. It seemed impossible to prove that one of them must be lying. Then Solomon called for a sword and ordered the child to be cut in two and divided between the women. Immediately one of the women said that rather than have the child killed, she would give up her claim. Solomon realised that this was true mother love and ordered that the child should be given to this woman.

The report of Solomon's shrewdness in settling an apparently insoluble problem was quickly noised abroad. It was exactly the shrewdness which delighted the ancient world and would be embodied in a folk tale. Solomon acquired a reputation for this kind of proverbial wit and wisdom. The authorship of many proverbs was attributed to him, so too were many poems and a veritable literature of wise sayings. He was Solomon the magnificent, the man who built and adorned with gold the Temple (and his palace which was considerably larger), who had the largest harem and the most superb stables. His fame spread throughout the nations.

2. *The last analysis*

But when Solomon's reign came to an end, the man and his policies were mercilessly exposed. To pay for his style and ostentation, the whole country had endured an unbearable load of taxation. He had treated his own region of Judah so much more favourably than the ten tribes of the north, that the latter were on the point of rebellion. When Solomon's reckless son Rehoboam refused to lighten their burdens, they set up a rival kingdom and would have eliminated the still loyal region of Judah, if Rehoboam had not won the help of Egypt. And the price was a large part of the wealth, including the gold of the palace and the temple, which his father had amassed. That was the end of the national dream of a world empire based upon the great potential of the kingdom which David had left to his son, the son who had been given an understanding heart but had let it wither away.

3. What went wrong?

There is an old Spanish proverb which runs: 'God says, take what you want and pay for it.' This may sound like a rather grim discouragement to prayer but it is in fact only summing up a part of human experience. We tend to decide for ourselves what we need from God without considering what might be the full consequences of our request if it were granted. We obtain that new job on which we have set our heart. When it goes wrong, this is usually either because it brings with it problems which we never tried to foresee, or because we ourselves are unable to measure up to the demands which it makes on us.

God's condition to Solomon was meant to be his safeguard. But Solomon ignored it. He brought in foreign wives each importing her own brand of religion. He discontinued his father's principle of acting as king by covenant and saw himself as an absolute monarch. He rejected the ideal of religion which later the prophet Micah summed up so superbly in these words: 'What doth the Lord require of thee, but to do justly, and to love mercy, and to walk humbly with thy God?' Humility would have been anathema to a king so bent on creating a grand impression.

It is indeed one of the curiosities of religious literature that so many serious and deep enquiries into the nature of true wisdom should have attached to the reputation of a king who was without wisdom in the true sense of the word.

4. What is wisdom?

The search for true wisdom runs through much of the Old Testament. The writers thought of it at two levels. One was the 'prudential' level of sound principles which should be put into practice in daily life and relationships. They were not interested in expediency and compromise but they made plenty of allowance for the frailty of human nature. They asked people to take a long term view of life and to look at the means as well as the ends.

The other level was one of reflection on life in general. Here one must admit that the writers were usually somewhat pessimistic about human wisdom. Indeed, some took the view that life itself could be futile seeing that human nature was so largely incapable of rational and responsible behaviour. So they believed that only in relation to God could man find true wisdom and live by it. Their main principle was, as in Proverbs 1.7, that 'The fear of the Lord is the beginning of wisdom'.

5. The fear of the Lord?

If there is one phrase that has disappeared from the contemporary Christian vocabulary, it is 'the fear of the Lord'. We have caricatured it in an image of a grovelling worshipper scared of the power of a vengeful and unpredictable deity. We have turned the love of God into the sentimentality of a father who would never presume to direct, let alone correct, his children even when he knows they are heading for trouble.

But what these Old Testament writers had in mind was the filial fear, the respect and regard of the Son for the Father, which was exemplified in Jesus himself. Jesus never took God for granted, in the wrong sense of that phrase. He demonstrated the true wisdom both at the practical level of conduct and relationships, and at the level of broad principle which was the Kingdom of God in action. Justice and mercy, righteousness and love, were all part of the true wisdom.

This is not as distant from our contemporary situation as some might think. The most widespread demand in the world is for security and justice. Men are less and less sure that they will receive these from the plans and policies of the so-called wise men of our time. They are overwhelmed by the spate of advice, opinions, analyses, reports and manifestos, all claiming infallibility and most of them contradicting each other. So few give evidence of the reverent agnosticism of the man who does not claim to know the whole truth—even about himself!

Neither can the Church claim to know the whole truth and to have the true wisdom, least of all if it leaves God out of account in making its decisions, or in its ministry to the world whose very existence the writer of Prov. 3.19 saw as due to the wisdom of God. But both the Church and the Christian can pray as Solomon did for the gift of the understanding heart. That understanding has to begin with the awareness of God, in His world and in the people who live in it. It has to be sustained by that walking with God which could have saved Solomon from himself.

PERSONAL EXPERIENCE

God's builders (Nehemiah)

Among the Old Testament records there are stories of people whose outstanding intelligence and powers of analysis bear comparison with anything we boast about in our own era. One such is Nehemiah, a Jewish leader of the post-exilic period, whose shear brilliance is almost unparalleled in the Bible.

1. *The call to the exile*

We first meet Nehemiah when he holds one of the most important and dangerous posts in the Persian court. He is cup-bearer to King Artaxerxes. Attempted assassination was an occupational hazard of monarchy in those days. Poisoning the king's food or drink was an easy method of accomplishing this, if one could bribe the man who was cup-bearer and wine-taster. Nehemiah, a Jewish exile, seems to have won the confidence of the King and been appointed to this job.

One day the King remarks on his cup-bearer's sadness of countenance. Nehemiah explains that he has had bad news from home, telling him of the devasted state of his city of Jerusalem which had been conquered by the Babylonians in 586 B.C. and was now being despoiled by the neighbouring tribesmen. The King gives him permission to return. He can take with him some friends and orders for supplies to be given by local officers responsible for the area. So, leaving his comfort and security in exile, Nehemiah returns to Jerusalem.

2. *The survey and the plan*

In the year 444 B.C. Nehemiah arrived and made contact with the local authorities who were not particularly pleased to see him. He found the position worse than he had expected. With a handful of trusted friends he made a tour of the ruined city.

There were four alternatives before him. One was of course to do nothing, and to return to the security of the Court. Another was to do the pious thing and rebuild the Temple. A third, to start by rebuilding the homes of the people, would have been a politically popular move. But Nehemiah decided that to build the wall around the entire city was the first priority. When that was achieved, the rest could follow later.

3. Building by families

Instead of concentrating his labour force on one section of the wall at a time, Nehemiah determined to attempt to build the whole length of the wall simultaneously. He assigned a portion to every family to work side by side. Because of the danger of attack from the neighbouring tribesmen, Nehemiah commanded the builders to retain their weapons with half of the people on guard at any given time. Despite these difficulties, the wall began to rise for 'the people had a mind to work' (Nehemiah 4.6).

4. Personal attack

When the local chieftains had failed to impede the building on the wall by direct attack and attempts at a fifth column, they realised at last that their main attack should have been upon Nehemiah himself. So they invited Nehemiah to come and discuss the whole matter with them at a village in 'neutral' territory. But he realised that this was only an attempt to get him away from the city and assassinate him. He replied 'I am doing a great work, so that I cannot come down.' They tried one last trick, to threaten to report to the Persian overlord that Nehemiah was trying to establish his own kingdom. But he remained firm and the wall was completed, so the Temple could be rebuilt and the housing of the people could be commenced.

5. Assessing the problem

This narrative of Nehemiah's leadership starts with his acceptance of personal responsibility. He did not bewail the situation and feel that someone else ought to do something about it. He accepted it as his problem. This in itself is not easily achieved in any church or community if its members have become accustomed to uninvolved membership. The first stage of missionary endeavour tends to pass to a stage of passive membership which is reluctant to continue to make the same effort and sacrifice as that of the pioneers. The members cease to see themselves in a frontier situation; the frontier is always moving on. They let themselves be overwhelmed by the size and extent of their problems and need to analyse them realistically. In the parish situation, we have to make ourselves aware of both the problems and the resources available. We have to recognise as Nehemiah did that with God nothing is impossible. But we have also to follow his example in choosing the right priority, and shaping our activities in accordance with it. For instance if the basic need of a church is considered to be its spiritual renewal, or the education of its members, or the development of its fellowship or a new outreach to the community, then this must be the focal point of its planning. To do as many of us do, just muddling along trying to do everything at once, can be wasteful and calamitous.

6. *The family is the salient of the Church*

It is interesting that the wall of Jerusalem was built, as later the local churches were to be established, by families. St Paul's letters usually end with greetings to the 'households' of many members. We know that they were 'given to hospitality' which the Apostles could count on in their travels as could any Christians moving from one city to another. But this was more than a social exercise. The home was the salient of the Church—it was the area of support for the baptised and confirmed, the married and the aged and the sick and bereaved. It was the real 'extended family' which first made contact with the world outside.

All that was centuries ago. Yet today the Christian family has a significance no less important to the Church. To quote but one example, it is a fact that many youngsters from broken homes, who have never experienced stability and affection in family life, have been welcomed to experience it in Christian families. There they have learned something of what marriage and parenthood can be like at their best. This is not a sentimental glamorizing of a situation. It really does happen. In one's parochial experience one has come to value immensely the contribution of such families not only to the Church but also to the community as a centre of concern and care. 'The church that is in their house', of Romans 16.5, is an apt description of such a family. This is where the Church's teaching on marriage and family life is seen not as a statement of doctrine and theory but as a positive contribution to the life of every family and to the stability of every marriage.

7. *The meaning of vocation*

But to accomplish this asks of everyone of us the kind of dedication which Nehemiah was revealing in his refusal to come down to the level of his enemies. Without any 'holier-than-thou' superiority, the Christian has to face the possibility of taking a definite stand at times on matters of conviction. His first responsibility to the call of God is to fulfil his commitment which began at his baptism, was strengthened at his confirmation, grows through his life by prayer and sacrament and by obedience to the Word of God, and is sustained in the fellowship of his church. Like Martin Luther, he has to say 'I can do no other' if he is to be true to his very integrity. For vocation means a call to holiness and to wholeness, to experience the vision of God on the Mount of Transfiguration which one can take down into the valley beneath, where men can have a chance of responding 'Lord, I believe, help thou mine unbelief.'

PERSONAL EXPERIENCE

The pillar of the Church (Barnabas)

The Generation Gap receives so much attention that one might be excused for thinking it to be a modern phenomenon and a dangerous one at that. But there has always been a gap between successive generations and it is not altogether a bad thing. If it did not exist, then society would be static and there would be no development as one age succeeded another.

Its real problem nowadays is that differences in outlook, in educational and economic level, and in social patterns between old and young are probably greater than they were previously. They can cause tensions and conflict through failure in communication and understanding, on both sides. The way to bridge the gap is exemplified in the New Testament in the contribution of a Christian who came to be known as Barnabas. His name means 'The son of consolation' or, in modern terms, 'the persuader'. In Acts 11.24, he has the superb testimonial of being 'a good man, and full of the Holy Spirit and of faith'.

1. *The man who took risks*

He began his Christian life as Joseph, a Jew from Cyprus, who sold up his possessions and brought the proceeds into the communal pool of the infant church. He was just an ordinary member of the congregation and was not even one of the seven appointed deacons, but his judgement came to be respected. When Paul, after his conversion, tried to join the Jerusalem Christians, they were acutely suspicious of him. Paul might have been lost to the Church had not Barnabas given him the benefit of the doubt and persuaded the others to do the same.

The church spread to Antioch. Its success there among the Gentiles worried the Christians at Jerusalem. They sent Barnabas down to examine the situation. He encouraged the Antiochenes to go on with their mission. He then took the trouble to travel to Tarsus to bring Paul to help them and they spent a year there together.

Then it became clear that God was calling the Church to a new mission and this time overseas. Paul and Barnabas accepted the responsibility of this dangerous venture and took Barnabas' nephew, John Mark, with them as general helper. Although sometimes their lives were at risk, they achieved success in their mission.

Later St Paul decided it was time to revisit the churches founded on their first journey. Barnabas wanted to take John Mark with them again. Apparently the young man had been unable to face the dangers of the first journey and had deserted the two leaders. Barnabas wanted to give him a second chance. Paul would not agree. So the two Apostles parted company and this would make a sad end to their partnership but 1 Corinthians 9.6 suggests that they were subsequently reconciled. Both men were too great to harm the Church by personal disagreements.

2. *The pillars of the Church*

Every congregation owes much to those who like Barnabas have been 'pillars of the church'. But it can be a title with two aspects. Some who bear it have, understandably, carried the weight of leadership in the maintenance of their church. It is only natural if such people sometimes tend to be chiefly concerned about continuity, holding fast to tradition and suspicious of change. At worst, their introverted conservatism can contribute to the decline of the very thing they love.

Barnabas accepted the responsibility of involvement in extension as well as maintenance. His being a 'good man' was not the whole picture. He was also 'full of the Holy Spirit and of faith'. He was a man remarkable for what we now value highly as 'open-ness'. His mind was open to new demands and to new ideas about the nature of the Church and its mission. At the same time, his awareness of what was best in the traditional method and values enabled him to win the confidence of the more conservative elements in the Church of his time. Without his contribution at a particular time, the whole mission to the Gentiles might have been delayed for years.

3. Maintenance and mission

It may seem a platitude to say that the Church today faces a missionary situation in many ways comparable to that of the first century. It is called to go out to where people are and to meet their needs as they are now, not as they might have been years ago. It has to train itself to be a mobile Church of mobile members and mobile resources.

The tension between maintenance and mission has to be accepted as part of the essence of Christianity. They are not optional alternatives. They face us in the parochial situation which is the living context of our Apostleship. They face us in the share we carry of the burdens of the Church overseas. Our response to this dual commitment can be gauged from our parochial budget, from the extent to which our young people hear and respond to vocations to service as Christians in ministry within the Church or in the community. Dare we ask our own congregation when it last produced an ordinand or a missionary? Dare we ask what support we give to those of our members who are engaged in occupations of service to people in the local area?

The genius of Barnabas lay in his understanding of both parts of the Church's vocation and his willingness to be involved in each of them. They called him 'A good man, full of the Holy Spirit and of faith'. These were his three outstanding characteristics, each of them not static but dynamic, lively and responsive to the call of God and to the needs of man. His was the kind of Christianity which can build bridges between generations and between nations.

PERSONAL EXPERIENCE

The first Christian in Europe (Lydia)

The first person in Europe we know of to become a Christian was a woman. She was a business woman living in Philippi, on the mainland of Greece. We are not certain of her name. In Acts 16.14, the Authorised Version calls her Lydia. But this is more likely to mean that she was known as The Lydian because she came from a district of that name in Asia Minor, which we now know as Turkey. She was a seller of purple, that is, a commercial agent for purple-dyed clothes from Thyatira, and she played a vital part in the outreach of the Church.

She appeared at a critical time. In obedience to a vision in the night of a man from Macedonia appealing for help, Paul and his companions, Luke, Silas and Timothy, had sailed across to the port of Neapolis. Possibly they expected to find a ready audience. But there was none. They went on to the important Roman colony of Philippi. Again, nothing happened. There was no synagogue in which the Apostle could make his first contacts as he usually did.

So on the sabbath he went down to the river bank outside the city. There he might meet Philippian Jews fulfilling their obligations of ritual washing. He found some women and spoke to them. They might have been Jewish, or Gentiles interested in Judaism. One of them responded to St Paul's teaching. It was Lydia. She listened, weighed up what the Apostle taught and decided on the spot to become a Christian. She was baptised and so was her household.

Then she looked at the Apostle and his three friends with womanly compassion. She might have thought that they could do with a square meal or to have someone to do their washing for them. Tactfully she suggested that they would be welcome to stay in her house. In fact, she insisted on their doing so.

Thus began the church at Philippi, the one to which later St Paul could write his most joyous Epistle.

1. *The businesslike approach*

It is not without significance that the first Christian in Europe was a business woman, accustomed to earning her living the hard way in a foreign country, and experienced in assessing the quality of goods and of the people she had to deal with. Like many other 'God-fearers', she had probably been attracted to Judaism by its faith in the One God and by its high ideals of personal and family life. Now she was offered something better and accepted it. Unlike the Athenians who were later to hear the Apostle and to say merely 'Very interesting. We must talk about this again some time', she made her decision. She took the Church into her home and offered her home to the Church.

2. Faith and grace

There has been much argument about the once-for-all decision in Christian membership. Some people, like St Paul, look back to one crucial moment. Others take the view that membership can start almost imperceptibly even with the kind of habitual Christianity that begins with childhood in a 'Church' home. They emphasise the development aspect of membership, seeing it as a growth in grace and fellowship and sacrament. Both views can be right. But each can be wrong if it denies the validity of the other. Neither is complete without the other. The 'twice-born' Christian who looks back to a single crucial event can remain perilously static in his religion and unable to appreciate that for some people a very different experience can be equally valid. On the other hand, the 'gradual' Christian can drift into an equally static religion which never makes any decision.

The world is not particularly interested in this distinction. It feels that Christians can be known by their fruits rather than by their interpretations of religious experience. We witness by our lives more than by our words. And that witness must begin as it did with Lydia, with our homes, for they are the shop-windows of the Church.

3. Both . . . and . . .

The Church has to be a fellowship of both faith and grace, of decision and of growth. Under the pressure of events, through which God Himself may well be working, many of the old distinctions are being seen to be less relevant than they used to be. We are now more interested in seeing what we have in common and in bringing together the valid elements in different kinds of experience and tradition. The Church has to be Catholic in its value of ministry and sacrament, its sense of fellowship with the saints and martyrs, its awareness of unity between the Church past, present and future.

The Church has to be Pro-testant, in the literal sense of the word, in positive testimony to the value of the Bible, to the importance of individual responsibility and to the inescapable obligation to evangelise.

From the international level to the local parish, we are being called to a new open-ness to the Gospel, and to say, as Lydia did, 'If you have judged me to be faithful to the Lord, come into my house and abide there.'

PERSONAL EXPERIENCE

Law and order (Town Clerk of Ephesus)

If there was one thing which the Town Clerk of Ephesus dreaded more than anything else, it was a riot. Not that he was afraid of a mob, but he feared that if it got out of control it would give the Roman authorities an excuse to suspend local government and impose martial law. That very nearly happened and it was because of a clash between Christianity and Commerce.

The account of this in Acts 19 starts with a protest meeting organised by one Demetrius, the self-appointed leader of the silversmiths. Their main business was making images of Diana, the goddess of the Ephesians, for the tourist trade.

His speech was a masterpiece of rabble-rousing. He told his fellow-workers that their trade, on which their very living depended, was being threatened by the spread of the Christian teaching that man-made gods were useless. He put a pious gloss on his appeal to self-interest by expressing concern lest the great goddess should lose her status.

The crowd reacted predictably. They swarmed into the amphitheatre which could house 24,000 people and went on shouting protests and slogans for some hours.

Then the Town Clerk came on to the stage. He assured the audience that the reputation of Diana was not in danger—after all, he asked them, did not the city possess her very image which had come down from heaven? He said that if Demetrius had a valid complaint he could take it to the courts or even to the Council, where justice would be done. Then he pointedly reminded them that there was a serious risk of Roman punishment for this kind of riotous assembly.

The crowd dispersed. But the situation remained so dangerous that St Paul, whose effective preaching had caused the commotion, was persuaded to leave the city secretly. So Ephesus, the capital of the Roman province of what we now call Turkey, lost the opportunity of becoming a centre of Christianity.

1. *The appeal of the demagogue*

Demetrius and the Town Clerk typify two forces which are repeatedly in conflict. Demetrius is the demagogue who rocks the boat himself and persuades the passengers that there is a storm at sea. He uses high-flown statements of principle to disguise his appeal to fear and insecurity. The last thing he wants is that they should use their reason. When he persuades them to follow his way of self-interest, he helps them to feel a golden glow of noble purpose.

He knows that in such situations men tend to behave like a herd. The individual finds it well nigh impossible to stand apart and weigh up the pros and cons of the problem. He ceases to think of the opponents as people, human beings like himself. They become caricatures to be despised and hated.

This is the situation which George Orwell forecast in '*1984*' and '*Animal Farm*' as a logical development of present tendencies. It has occurred before, in the history of nations and tribes. It has even happened in the history of the Church as, for instance, in the wars of the Reformation and Counter-Reformation. In the name of Christianity men have destroyed each other. But it has been their own brand of Christianity, not Christ's. God made man in His own image. Man returns the compliment by making God in man's image.

2. *The appeal to reason*

Man likes to think of himself as a rational being. But in a crisis, his reason can be overcome by his emotions. The Town Clerk shrewdly appealed to both, scaring them with the threat of a military take-over, but also treating them as responsible citizens.

His main argument on the particular problem before them was to stress the importance of law and order. If they wanted justice then the courts were open to them. This was not a mere expedient. It was basic to the life of the community and the Empire. The Romans gave their subject peoples stable government. They strove to maintain the Pax Romana. Within that protection of peace, commerce and industry, learning and literature, could flourish. Without it, everything was in jeopardy.

St Paul was well aware of this. He could write in Romans 13 in praise of 'the powers that be' because he appreciated that at that time the State was neutral towards Christianity, which could therefore move fairly freely about the world. But later in the New Testament period Rome changed its policy to one of persecution.

3. *The foundation of society*

The priority of law and order tends to be obscured. If we were asked what is the most important element in the life of the community, we might answer in terms of health, education, industry, commerce or housing. But without law and order, not one of these can exist for long. To experience the full advantages of a free society, we need the safeguards of justice without corruption, government which preserves liberty rather than licence, and constructive protection against crime and violence.

All this we take for granted until we are in danger of losing it. And it can be lost when the Demetrius approach succeeds. This happens when people cease to care about good government and when government itself becomes remote from the people.

4. *The Christian Responsibility*

Christians believe that the Gospel provides valid standards by which priorities for both the citizen and the State can be assessed. It teaches that the real purpose of law and order is that men can be free to live as God intended them to live. It holds that governments, like individuals, are accountable to God.

If this is only theory kept in a vacuum, then it is not likely to have much effect in the situations where decisions are taken.

The hard fact is that the 'witness' of the Church is not much use without 'witnesses'. What a man does personally to preserve law and order, to play a part in government, to participate where decisions are made in politics or industry or commerce or education—it is by his action here that the Christian brings the Gospel to bear upon the life of the community.

Some of us are inhibited from fulfilling this because we have an antiquated idea that this is not 'Church Work'—as if that were confined to the interior life of the Church, ranging from polishing the brass to sitting on ecclesiastical committees. But Church Work is also the Work of the Church outside in the world, in the Ephesian amphitheatres of today.

PERSONAL EXPERIENCE

The letter that changed a life (Philemon)

Have you ever received a letter that changed your life? It might have contained the offer of a job, the result of an examination, or tidings of a death. It might indeed have seemed unimportant at the time and its significance only became apparent later. But what really mattered was not so much the message as your reponse to it.

This was so in the case of a man who received a letter which put unexpectedly and squarely before him the cost of discipleship. His name was Philemon and St Paul was the writer of what is the most personal letter in the New Testament.

1. *The message arrives*

Imagine Philemon at Colossae, a small town in what we now know as Turkey. He was a true pillar of the local church, supporting its leaders, generous and compassionate to the poor. He was probably happy except for one thing. He hated to be let down by people and this had happened to him through a young slave whom he had educated and treated well. The young fellow had stolen some of his master's property. Philemon's business associates would give him little sympathy. They would say he had been a fool to take so much trouble over the slave. They would advise him to exercise his legal rights and have the fellow put to death as a runaway slave and a thief, if ever he laid hands on him again.

A knock on the door—and there stands the runaway slave, white-faced and trembling with fear. He holds out a parchment roll and stammers something about Paul. Philemon seizes the parchment and sees at the end of it the signature of the Apostle himself. He wonders what possible connection there could be between this young rascal and the great Apostle. For Paul had made Philemon a Christian and he owed everything to him.

2. *The challenge of the letter*

In the letter, St Paul pleads for the young man Onesimus (his name means The Helpful One) who ran away, got into further trouble and landed up in prison. There he has met the Saint—and become a Christian.

Gently the Apostle reminds Philemon of his indebtedness to him for his conversion, but he does not press this. It is Philemon's indebtedness to God which is the real issue. It is in the light of this that Paul feels he can ask Philemon to take the slave back and to forgive him. Furthermore he asks the master to go a step further and to receive Onesimus as a brother in Christ. As to the money stolen, Paul himself will make this good when he comes. He concludes by expressing confidence that Philemon will consent.

The existence of the letter is evidence that Philemon agreed. He would surely have destroyed it if he had decided to refuse Paul's request. So it became one of the treasures of the church at Colossae.

3. The cost of the Cross

What would you and I have done in the circumstances? We must realise that Philemon was being asked to fly in the face of law, custom and public opinion and to ignore his rights, thinking first and foremost of his obligations as a Christian. To forgive a slave was hard enough. To accept him as a brother was much more demanding. It would be like bridging the age-long gap between Jew and Samaritan, between Greek and barbarian, between black and white.

This simple incident is in fact bringing us up against the real challenge of the Gospel in the work of reconciliation. For it asks men to probe beneath differences of status or opinion to establish a new blood-relationship which means entirely new responsibilities. People sometimes criticise the early church, and Jesus too, for failing to denounce the institution of slavery which was so widespread in their time. But they were in fact going to the root of the matter by demanding that people should recognise a fundamental identity which transcended differences of class or status or race.

4. The personal test

So while the letter was challenging Philemon in respect of a particular relationship, it was also testing him in his life-situation. His whole value of the Gospel was being probed. This happens often in human experience. St Peter, for example, was confident that he would not betray Jesus. But the remark of a servant girl broke him. He was prepared for the big test, but not for the small one. To Philemon the challenge came in a letter. To us it may come in an apparently trifling incident, when we could speak but are silent, when we should act but do nothing, when we should show love but our concern for ourselves make us blind to the need of others.

St Paul could write to Philemon confident that he would make the right response because, as he wrote, 'We are both in Christ'. The secret lies in the practice of the presence of Jesus, that constant awareness of our Lord which means that when we are faced with a sudden test our first response will be one of truth and love.

We might sum this up ourselves in one question: 'What do you do when you don't know what to do?' Panic? Worry? Get Angry? Pray? Or do we ask what Jesus would do in this situation? What do *you* do?

PERSONAL EXPERIENCE

The teenage saint (Agnes)

The Christian Calendar commemorates an extraordinary company of Saints—active, contemplative, men, women, statesmen or hermits, of many nations and many generations. It seems a formidable company but there is at least one very delightful touch about it, in that it includes a teenager who lived in Rome in the 4th century. Her name was Agnes and she was martyred because even at the early age of thirteen she had decided on a life of chastity and of service to Jesus.

She was denounced by some other youngsters as an adherent of the Christian religion which at that time was proscribed. In the attempt to make her give way and renounce her religion she was offered inducements and threatened with torture. Neither had any effect on her constancy and so she was executed. The news of her self-sacrifice spread rapidly. Soon her martyrdom was being commemorated by Christians throughout the Roman Empire. For centuries it has been remembered daily in the Canon of the Roman Mass.

1. *The age of decision*

Some might dismiss this as one more example of 'religious mania' occurring in early adolescence, as a possible effect of puberty on the personality as well as the body. But this would be a superficial argument. This is the time of life when many young people come to make decisions, perhaps not always clearly seen so at the time, which have a lasting effect. At a recent missionary conference three speakers on furlough from overseas, an archbishop, a priest and a doctor, were asked at what age they had had their first awareness of the possibility of missionary service. Independently, each said that it was at about the age of thirteen.

It would be interesting to put this question about vocation to any of us in the ordained ministry or giving other full-time Christian service. Then we might go on to ask what circumstances at that time brought this awareness before us. In the case of St Agnes, it might have been the situation in her own church which was under daily threat of increased persecution. Even as a young girl she would have seen the challenge to the Christian witness of loyalty to Christ. The immorality of her time would also have made her aware of the need for a moral witness. Young people are naturally idealists but often they are more acutely aware of what is happening in the human environment than they are given credit for being.

2. *The response of youth*

A tablet three thousand years old bore an inscription. When translated this was found to say: 'Young people are not what they used to be'.

So the lament of the older generation about youth is not a novelty. Of course young people are not what they used to be. Neither is the life-situation in which they find themselves.

As compared with previous generations, they tend nowadays to be better educated than were their parents, to achieve economic independence and to mature physically at an earlier age.

They seem less likely than we were to accept uncritically the values and standards of their parents. This is not altogether a bad thing. One American University recently reported that its best graduates were refusing conventional forms of employment such as jobs in Father's Firm or ready-made professions with high pay and good prospects. They were rejecting the traditional goals of the three-car family with the swimming pool. Instead they were choosing employment at lower pay where they would be of service to under-privileged communities.

When questioned about this, many of them said that the traditional patterns of life did not seem to have brought their parents much happiness, or stable marriages or a meaningful life.

In its most extreme form, this refusal of youth to take the familiar path takes a negative form of withdrawal from responsible involvement in the total society. Living in self-centring communes, rejecting marriage, escaping into the world of drugs, associating in religious or occult cults—these are only some of the ways in which young people say 'No!' to life as their fathers have known it.

They may live on the society which they condemn, and be themselves condemned as parasites rather than producers. Often they are rejecting most of all the materialism of the community as a whole which can be quite unscrupulous in its commercial exploitation of youth, even while it professes altruism in the sacred cause of progress.

3. The response of youth

Young people, however, can show a remarkable capacity for helping to meet the needs of others particularly in community service to the aged. They can respond powerfully to definite calls to serve in some organisation, religious or otherwise, which make considerable demands upon them. In an age when experimental sex and violence are all too often characteristic of adult behaviour, they can follow their own codes of purity and self-control with remarkable dedication. In a time when much of their education is secularist, non-moral and job-orientated, the teenagers are still able to look at religion with appreciation, to be concerned about moral values that will really work, and to look for more meaning in life than only the earning of a living.

What all this would suggest is that neither those who are always critical of the young or those who confidently assert that 'there is nothing wrong with modern youth' do the situation justice.

As Christians we might ask ourselves whether our 'image' of youth accords with the facts or indeed what accuracy there is in our picture of what we were like when we were young. We might consider what kind of impression our own lives could be making on the young people with whom we are in contact, in a situation where what we are is more impressive than what we say. And we might think about the rebuke of Jesus to those who, consciously or unconsciously, would deter the young people and children from being where they belonged—in the presence of his love.

For over sixteen hundred years the Church has remembered with gratitude a teenager who gave her life for her faith. Agnes is herself a reminder to the Church to keep itself young in heart, to dare to dream dreams as well as to have visions.

PERSONAL EXPERIENCE

The 'human' saint (Aidan)

I received the following letter after a broadcast:

Dear Sir,

.I was very shocked to hear you say on the radio this morning that Christians ought to have a sense of humour and a sense of proportion. I think that because ministers of religion have been saying this kind of thing, the Devil is out and about and not where he ought to be, in the chains in the Abyss. Perhaps you too, Sir, are a limb of Satan.

I remain,
Your sincere friend . . .

1. *The Mote and the Beam*

That listener certainly took life seriously. But her unease about a sense of humour and a sense of proportion exemplified the censorious attitude which Christ himself condemned. He was speaking about people who busied themselves about other people's faults and ignored their own. Their blindness to their personal failings made it impossible for them to be of any real help to others. The absurdity of this situation he summed up in his caricature of a man with a plank in his eye offering to remove a speck of sawdust in his brother's eye.

This was one example of a profound and realistic tolerance which Jesus advocated not merely as an exercise in good relations but as essential to the relation of a man with God as well as with his neighbour. He expressed this in one terse command: Judge not. He went on to warn his hearers that they themselves would be assessed by the very same standard which they applied to others. That standard might be censorious and fault-finding and discouraging. Or on the other hand, it might reflect Christ's own compassionate understanding of a man's problems of personality and of the factors which had helped him to become what he was. This was not to be a blind ignoring of the existence of evil. Instead it was to be positive and hopeful and realistic.

2. *The saint who understood*

This characteristic of Christian discipleship was exemplified in a 7th century British saint who found himself charged with the responsibility of evangelising the north-east of England. Aidan was a monk of Iona. One of his associates was sent to help King Oswald in bringing Christianity to Northumbria. The mission was a failure and the monk blamed the Northumbrians for it. He reported that they were crude and hostile. Aidan suggested that the real fault had been in the approach of his colleague who had been giving his audiences what one might call 'A-level' material beyond their comprehension and irrelevant to their lives as they had to live them. The result of giving this advice was that Aidan found himself asked to take over the work.

With the Holy Island of Lindisfarne as his base, Aidan made long journeys throughout the huge area of which he was now Bishop, supporting the Christian communities and forming new ones. This he did for 17 years. Far from regarding the people of the area as of little potential, Aidan selected from them a dozen boys whom he carefully trained to become the future leaders of the Church and nation. One of them was Chad, the saintly Bishop of Mercia.

Aidan believed in God. He also believed in people. Because they knew he was a man of integrity and a man who cared about them, they were willing to accept his Gospel.

3. The question of judgement

It is undoubtedly true that Christianity has acquired a reputation for censoriousness through the centuries. Its Gospel has been regarded as a catalogue of 'Don'ts' rather than as a positive message of 'Do's'. This is perhaps inevitable when the witness of the Church has so often had to call men away from ways of life likely to lead to disaster and call them to a way of self-denial and high moral standard. Too often all this has seemed to be world-denying to an unnecessary extent and seeming to ignore the fact that the world is after all the creation of God. It is also true that the Church within its own fellowship has been slack about living up to its own standard. It has been much more anxious about the liturgical obligations of its members than their ethical responsibilities. It has found it easier to be devoted to the Saints than to try to imitate them.

Contemporary thought goes in the opposite direction. It says that it is wrong to judge men's conduct without making allowances for all the circumstances including the psychological and social, which can have a bearing on that conduct. This is not really in conflict with the teaching of Jesus. He refused to take conventional attitudes of judgement about such people as prostitutes and publicans. He saw into their hearts and he understood their circumstances. That did not in any way weaken his clear definition of right and wrong and his concern for truth. It was by this double criterion of truth and compassion that he wanted his disciples to make judgements about the world and about themselves.

4. *The true tolerance*

To achieve this sense of proportion in our judgements is not easy. Criticism is always easier to give others than to apply to ourselves. Sometimes our criticism of our neighbour is an unconscious attempt to divert attention from our own failings and to quieten our conscience. Psychology suggests that when our censoriousness is extreme it may be because we are secretly tempted by the very sins we so bitterly condemn.

If censoriousness is a manifestation of insecurity in personal life, it is equally so in the life of the community. There is a curious confusion between tolerance of evil in many forms, and readiness to delight in scandal. The 'exposure' of greatness as an idol with feet of clay has become a literary industry. The spate of political autobiographies could not have been better designed if the primary intention of some of them was that of destroying faith in the possibility of political integrity and truly responsible government. As a community we are reluctant to give anyone the benefit of the doubt and a real second chance, particularly if he has become a criminal, even through no fault of his own. Yet we are willing to give a quite different tolerance towards those whose faults are protected by their power and status. The judgement of the community is variable and inconsistent and therefore people lose faith in it.

Yet where the judgement of Jesus was concerned, people came to have confidence in it. The disciples, for example, included two men, Simon the Zealot and Matthew the Publican, who came in with as much mutual hostility as that of one of the Resistance movement living alongside a Nazi during the last war. Nevertheless they learned to find unity in Christ and to judge each other by his standard.

And this is where all judgement must begin, with self judgement in the presence of Jesus whose truth and love reflects the judgement of God Himself.

PERSONAL EXPERIENCE

The whole man (Bede)

THE TOP PEOPLE

What makes someone internationally famous? It can be almost anything—political power, scientific achievement, success in the world of entertainment or even outstanding villany! The Press, Radio and Television can make him or her a household name in every continent. But such fame rarely lasts long. Today's star usually turns out to be a soon-forgotten comet.

Centuries ago communication between nations was slow and difficult. Yet there were people whose names became household words in many countries and visitors came immense distances to consult them. The reason was, strangely enough, their holiness.

Outstanding among them was a saintly scholar named Bede. He lived in Jarrow in the north of England from 673 to 735. His reputation attracted people from all over Europe. He was in fact the only Englishman mentioned by Dante in his *Paradiso*. He was given the unique title of 'The Venerable', a token of affection as well as respect. He was later described by another English Saint, Boniface, as 'The candle of the Church, lit by the Holy Spirit'.

1. *Bede the scholar*

From the age of seven until his death, Bede spent almost all his life in the monastery at Jarrow. But nothing could be further from the truth than the idea that Bede lived in cloistered seclusion from the outside world. He devoted himself to the study of the Scriptures and wrote about forty books, scientific, biblical and historical. His *Ecclesiastical History of the English People* is one of the most important source-books for subsequent study. Incidentally he introduced into this country the method of dating events of history as B.C. and A.D. He also enjoyed writing poetry.

2. *The scholar who cared*

Throughout his life Bede's scholarship was set in a double context —the vertical and the horizontal. The Daily Offices and the Sacraments, Communion and Prayer were the nourishment of his soul.

From his worship flowed his deep concern for people. He had a warm pastoral concern for the clergy and laity who faced the rigours of life in the dangerous world of the eighth century. Bede saw a close relation between his scholarship and the lives of the people. He would have regarded with astonishment the suggestion made often in our era that scholarship, science, art or music can be thought of as self-sufficient, to be pursued without reference to their relation to the community as a whole.

3. *The whole man*

Bede exemplified the truth that a person is a whole man and cannot be departmentalised. It is quite possible to pay lip service to this while in practice denying it completely, as we tend to do today.

The world of politics, for instance, occasionally rocks with some scandal. A well-known figure is shown to have more than the usual share of human frailty in the form of moral lapse, corruption or the like. There is much publicity and pressure for his resignation.

Immediately there are heard voices arguing that people in positions of great responsibility have a right to a private life however amoral that may turn out to be. Any who dare to think otherwise are dubbed narrow-minded and hypocritical.

What seems to be suggested here is that a man's public life bears little relation to his private life, as if the two could be kept separate within himself. Now when we look at this away from an atmosphere of sensation and apply it to our own ordinary lives, we see that the principle of departmentalising does not work. We all have to handle a set of different relationships simultaneously. A man may be at the same time a son, husband, father, citizen, member of a political party, employee or employer, or member of a church. Each association may make a different call upon his loyalty and his time. There may well be a conflict of duties and obligations. His happiness, indeed his very sanity, may depend upon his being able to deal with these varying commitments. What he cannot do is to behave like a number of different people living in separate rooms. He has to be one person with one basis for his values of himself and of others. This is what Jesus meant when he spoke of 'letting your eye be single and then your whole body is full of light.'

The key word is 'light', as it was for the Venerable Bede. He lived with an inner light which illuminated his relationships. So must we. For behind the façade of the famous 'personality', the career woman who handles her job and home and contacts, and behind the outward lives of ordinary folk like ourselves, there is the one person. He has to live with himself in the small room of solitude. There only God can integrate the real self and give us the light by which, in Matthew Arnold's words, we can 'see life steadily and see it whole'.

PERSONAL EXPERIENCE

Englishman in Europe (Boniface)

Which Englishman had the deepest influence on the history of Europe? According to one well-known historian, he was not a politician, scientist or inventor, but an English Saint who lived 1200 years ago. Born in Crediton and named Winfrid, he was later known as Boniface. He was largely responsible for converting Germany to Christianity and for liberating the Church in France from corruption and chaos.

There are many lives of St Boniface. Some emphasise his extraordinary efficiency in ecclesiastical organisation. But all agree that he stands out in holiness and warm attractiveness of personality. Because of his infectious enthusiasm he was able to recruit many young monks and nuns for the mission to Europe. He was always willing to hand over to a promising young disciple a share of his own responsibility. In modern terms, Boniface excelled in personnel selection, delegation and leadership.

His firmness of purpose was remarkable. From early youth he felt called to be a missionary. From this vocation he would not be diverted by success in other fields or by the failure of his first attempt to evangelise on the Continent. When any ordinary man might have felt entitled to relax after his great work in Germany and France, at the age of seventy-three Boniface went back as a missionary to the dangerous region of Friesland. In 754 he was martyred there.

1. *A man of courage*

The best-known story of Boniface tells of his courage when faced with the bitter hostility of paganism. A great crowd of heathen worshippers stood around their sacred oak. When Boniface attacked it with an axe, the watchers were convinced that the pagan gods would punish his sacrilege. Boniface split the oak asunder, and nothing happened. The people recognised that their gods were powerless even to defend their sanctuaries. From that day, evangelism went ahead. Boniface's conduct on this occasion was typical of his consistent disregard for personal safety when God's work had to be done.

2. The motive of mission

The Saint's name means literally 'Do Good'. He believed that doing good meant showing people the light of the Gospel, for their own souls' sake and not merely for the sake of the Church. The coming of Christianity brought with it a good measure of civilisation, with law and order and education.

This was also true of later missionary extension, as for example in the early nineteenth century. In many countries medical work, education, literacy and agricultural development started from the mission hospitals and schools. There many of the leaders of self-governing countries of Africa and Asia began their education.

It is undeniable that there was another side to the story of missions. In some areas missions went along with colonial expansion and commercial exploitation. Sometimes native customs and religious practices were suppressed because they were thought to be sinful. Nowadays many of these are valued differently because they are seen in their relation to the social structures of the local population. The missions have learned a deeper understanding of the significance of other religions. Instead of importing 'western' ways of worship and church life, they have pioneered in indigenisation, using the ways of expressions natural to the region. They have also readily handed over leadership to the people of the country.

What has been happening is a return to the basic motive of mission as pioneers like Boniface saw it. That motive was an essentially religious care for souls, coupled with a concern for the whole man in his total situation. Both care and concern arose from commitment to a faith which gave mission its content and its purpose. That faith compelled them to evangelise in spite of difficulties which were far more formidable than those which we encounter today.

3. The faith of the mission

Men and women like Boniface believed that as Christians they were under obligation to proclaim Christianity whatever might be the state of the Church at home or the opposition facing them. They preached a four-square Christianity of the Person of Christ, the Work of Christ, the Teaching of Christ, and the Body of

Christ—the Church. They wanted to share with others their experience that Jesus was the Way, the Truth and the Life.

Those three words which our Lord used of himself are of the utmost importance. The idea embodied in each of them is one of dynamic movement. The Way gives direction and guidance to life. The Truth is the confident venture from the revelation of Christ out into the world where God is constantly revealing new facets of His activity. The Life means supremely all that gives our own lives meaning—growth, achievement, relationships and purpose.

To mankind when it has lost its way, does not know where to look for truth, and finds life meaningless, this is the Gospel of the Christ who is the light of the world.

EDUCATION SUNDAY

The king who forgot (Alfred)

It is strange that one of the greatest Christians in English history should be best remembered for a fit of absent-mindedness. All that most of us know about King Alfred the Great is that he let the cakes burn when his hostess asked him to look after them. He had every excuse for being preoccupied. For the first seven years of his reign, which began in 871, he was battling against the Danes who overran almost the whole of his country. He and a few supporters were driven into hiding in the woods of Somerset.

When he let the cakes burn, Alfred would not have been thinking only about the Danes. He had great plans for the nation. When he established peace, he put these into effect. Alfred instituted a comprehensive system of laws. He reorganised the army and began building a navy. He started a record of the nation's history.

But his greatest work was in education. The clergy and nobles had become illiterate. So the King set up a school in his own palace. He brought to it scholars from Britain and Europe. His own son attended this school and Alfred himself learned Latin in order to translate great classics into English and make them generally available.

As a result of his leadership the nation defeated the Danes. Many of them actually became converts to Christianity and the foundations of national unity were laid.

Other kings and emperors in world history have been called 'Great'. None has been more deserving of the title as warrior, statesman and law-giver. In addition, Alfred was great in the wholeness of his concern for every aspect of the life of the nation. Not least in importance was his concern for education.

1. *What is education for?*

The King gave high priority to education. He believed that however essential was the defence of the realm and the establishment of law and order, no less important was education in the development of the country. In addition, Alfred believed that religious teaching and its values were necessary elements in the content of a whole education.

This vision of education has waxed and waned during subsequent centuries. Even at the beginning of the nineteenth century it was not thought to be the responsibility of the whole nation, so it was done by the churches or not done at all. Only slowly did the State accept any obligation. Even then a functional evaluation of it persisted. There was strong resistance to educating children for more than their 'station in life', as rural peasants or industrial workers. This idea is not confined to this country. In 1954 the South African Government compelled the churches to hand over the education of the Bantu so that young Africans should not be trained for rôles competitive with those which were the prerogative of the white population. Even today we are under pressure to shape education to fit young people for specific rôles in a technological civilisation.

We have to answer the question of the purpose of education with the individual in sight as well as his society. It is a necessity, and not merely an ideal, to define its purpose as that of helping him to be mature and intelligent, capable of thinking for himself and of acting responsibly, able to handle personal relationships and to acquire a sound set of values. We can hardly claim to be doing this everywhere when we still produce a dangerously large proportion of illiterates and youngsters whose way of life is one of frustration or of violence.

2. *The meaning of partnership*

The fact is, as Alfred realised, that education is a partnership between child, parent, teacher, school, community—and God. If one partner in that complex fails, or is not allowed, to play a part then something goes wrong with the result. We have also to remember that education takes place within the whole context of the community. We forget this when we blame the school for its apparent failures. The child and the school may be set in a social environment of unrest and materialism, and a society in which moral permissiveness and economic acquistiveness are dominant factors. This can happen at any level of the community.

The miracle is that despite these difficulties so very many of our young people become mature and responsible adults. That they do so is largely due to the encouragement of parents and the care of their teachers. These are the personal factors for which the most modern equipment and elaborate buildings cannot provide a substitute. For education is a relationship between people.

So when on 'Education Sunday' or at any other time we are offering special prayers about this, we are praying for all who share in this vitally important partnership which, as King Alfred saw clearly, is at the heart of the real welfare of the nation.